D0866424

# THE SASS MENAGERIE

*Robert L Steed* (signature)

# ROBERT L. STEED

*Illustrations by Jack Davis*

LONGSTREET PRESS

ATLANTA, GEORGIA

Published by
LONGSTREET PRESS, INC.
2150 Newmarket Parkway
Suite 102
Marietta, Georgia 30067

Printed in the United States of America

1st Printing, 1988

Library of Congress Catalog Card Number 88-081797

ISBN 0-929264-06-1

Design by Paulette Lambert
Cover Illustration by Jack Davis

Other Non-Pulitzer Prize Winners by Robert L. Steed

*Willard Lives!*

*Lucid Intervals*

*Money, Power, and Sex (A Self-Help Guide for All Ages)*

*To Joshua, Georgia and Nona Begonia, who,
despite all the parking tickets and
bank overdrafts, never fail to make
my heart smile*

—RLS

# Contents

# THE SASS MENAGERIE

# Surgeon General's Warning

The Surgeon General (I think it was the Surgeon General; he had a silly looking goatee and said he was a doctor) has issued a warning against buying a book and lending it to other people. According to him, the use of the same book by more than one person has caused the spread of grisly germs to a degree more dangerous than any other practice save sharing the same needle and, to use his words, "French kissing."

The Surgeon General also advises that over 80 percent of all cases of spousal violence occur after one partner to a marriage, while chuckling and snorting, attempts to read humorous passages from a book to the other partner when the other partner is attempting to sleep.

The message is clear. Share this book with no one. Make them (even spouses) buy one of their own. Is saving $14.95 (plus tax) worth a virulent disease or a violent beating? Think about it.

Thank you.

— RLS

# JOGGING CAUSES BRAIN DAMAGE

For the countless readers who look to me as a distant early warning system in the area of unwholesome trends, fetishes and aberrations in the social order, I am sorry to have to report that jogging, that persistent combination of masochism and exhibitionism, appears to be on the brink of giving birth to yet another sub-fad.

On Sunday last as I was weaving my automobile through the never-ending stream of sweaty joggers on Howell Mill Road on my way to obtain a nutritious sausage biscuit with cheese, I was jolted from my customary torpor by my wife's shrill exclamation, "Look at all those dumbbells!"

"It's just the usual spasm of Sunday morning joggers," I replied, trying to concentrate on my maneuvering and the sausage biscuit with cheese looming ever larger in my mind's eye.

"No," she said, "I'm talking about those things they're carrying in their hands while they run." Closer inspection revealed that my wizened companion was correct. About every fourth jogger seemed to be carrying what appeared to be an oversized pair of brass knuckles in each hand as he or she huffed and lurched through the public streets. (While we are on that subject, I think some legislation ought to be introduced requiring joggers to pursue their unsightly compulsion in places other than public thoroughfares. With the exception of drag racing and stealing hubcaps, I know of no other human pastime so monumentally arrogant that it presumes to preempt the public roads and byways to its own ends.)

Subsequent inquiry on my part revealed that the odd-looking devices being carried about by the joggers were specially configured weights called "Heavy Hands." In fact, some clinical material for further research surfaced in the person of my son, Joshua, who revealed that he had invested in a pair of Heavy Hands though he was unable to give me a satisfactory explanation as to their actual purpose.

Those who have been watching this sweaty social phenomenon develop over the years will quickly observe that there need be no valid purpose to create a jogging sub-fad. These poor souls whose brains have been systematically cauliflowered through years of sustained jogging have no capacity to resist the outrageous accoutrements relentlessly foisted on them by unscrupulous hucksters. Consider, for example, the terry-cloth elastic bands that joggers wrap about their heads and wrists; the specially designed jogging shoes themselves, each generation uglier than its predecessor, all resembling Hush Puppies with birth defects; the little radios with headsets to render joggers even more oblivious to oncoming traffic; the gym shorts worn, inexplicably, over and outside sweat pants; the atrocious velour pajama-type outfits with racing stripes, which increasing numbers of non-joggers have taken to wearing to shopping malls, grocery stores and picture shows; etc.; etc.

This latest fad began to take on sinister implications the more I pondered it. What, for example, had happened to the famous "Bird Man of Peachtree," who jogged along flapping his arms up and down in the manner of a gooney bird making an unscheduled landing? There had been no reported sightings of him for months. Had he perhaps become a victim of Heavy Hands?

Why, assuming there was some utilitarian purpose to be achieved by darting about in the public streets with these ridiculous appendages, couldn't the same result be achieved through the simple expedient of carrying a brick in each hand? (In fact, many bricks have mysterious holes in them which could well be adapted to just this end.) Were they designed and are they, in fact, being used as corrective devices for joggers with limp wrists? All of these seem to be questions worthy of broader consideration, and, while I have no answers at this point, I commend them to other interested parties for closer consideration.

I offer all this at some considerable personal risk for, as my wife so frequently points out, I have established a reputation (because of previous courageous public utterings) for being anti-physical fitness. While it is true that I once characterized the Peachtree Road Race as resembling "a stampede which would convince the unknowing that some sinister force had flushed everyone out of Cobb County in their underwear and was herding them south with electric cattle prods," and while I did have a cowcatcher welded to the front of my automobile as a lighthearted protest against the ever-increasing number of

joggers who clot the public streets and steadfastly refuse to yield the right of way to those who presume to use them for purposes as mundane as going back and forth to work or, on weekends, to fetch sausage biscuits with cheese, there is absolutely no basis to the widely held notion that I am anti-physical fitness. That proposition, I submit, is ridiculous on its face. After all, you're not born with a body like this. You have to work at it every single day.

*July 1985*

# A HARD DOG
# TO KEEP UNDER
# THE PORCH

Thursday, July 11, in the year of our Lord 1985, a date that will forever ring in history as the day the hostage crisis was finally resolved. And it was not a bunch of scruffy Shiite Muslims with terminal five o'clock shadow who broke the happy news to the swarming and frantic international press. Rather, it was a *troika* of dapper officials of the Coca-Cola Company who caused joy to reign from sea to shining sea with their announcement that the hostage, original-formula Coke, which had been held captive in the basement vault of the Trust Company Bank since April 23, was free at last and back on the streets as "Coca-Cola Classic."

Through a combination of officiousness, guile and sheer serendipity, this dilettante reporter managed to parlay a fortuitously timed luncheon engagement with a friend at Coke headquarters into an opportunity to be present at a newsbreak of such cosmic consequence that advance rumors of its nature caused debate in the United States Senate to be suspended and, even more incredible, caused ABC to break into *General Hospital* with the great glad tidings. I mean, when ABC risks interrupting Sean while he is secretly arranging for Robert to meet Holly in London or Derek's agreeing not to tell Mike that he's the boy's father, well, you know that something of intergalactic importance is afoot.

So, palming myself off as a reporter (I always keep a cheap, wrinkled suit and a battered felt hat with a press card in the band in the trunk of my car), I joined a gaggle of news gatherers in the Coca-Cola U.S.A. auditorium to hear the hosannas ring.

The good news was delivered by Coke Chairman Roberto Goizueta, whose beguiling accent makes you think of José Jiménez after four years at Yale, and Coke President Don Keough, whose rich Irish brogue and absolutely affidavit face would cause you not to be surprised if he suddenly started saying things like "Faith and Begorrah." (As an interesting aside, two of Mr. Keogh's six children, the twins, are named Faith and Begorrah.) This formidable Coke pair who, from a public relations standpoint probably represent the best one-two punch in corporate America, was joined by Coke U.S.A. President Brian Dyson, an Argentine who obviously understands American but speaks English with a trace of an Etonian accent.

The script was candid, direct and disarming and could have come straight out of a 1930s Frank Capra movie—Big Corporation makes big decision, little people all over America voice their displeasure, Big Corporation sees light (fade to swelling strains of "America the Beautiful" while camera pans up and away from Jimmy Stewart, the weary but now victorious spokesman for the Little Man).

The message these folks gave those embattled traditionalists who wanted the original formula Coke back was as simple and straightforward as the CB truckdriver's frequent rejoinder — "I heard *that.*"

Goizueta reaffirmed the company's commitment to new Coke but said Coca-Cola Classic would be brought back by popular demand. Keough said the passion of original Coca-Cola loyalists was a wonderful American mystery that caught them all by surprise, and he quoted bits from the avalanche of still-smoking mail:

> You have fouled up by changing the only perfect thing in this world. Before the courts fouled up the phone company, there were two perfect things. Now that you have changed Coca-Cola, there are none.

> Dear Chief Dodo (Keough said he passed this one along to Goizueta): What ignoramus decided to change the formula of Coke??? The new formula is gross, disgusting, unexciting and bad as Pepsi. Burn it!!!

And, speaking of brand X, the folks at Pepsi, whose ad campaign in response to the new Coke proved that the spirit of *Mommie Dearest* still lives, were reeling about the airwaves calling Coke the "Edsel of the 80s" and trying to decide whether the new news was good or bad. They must have decided the latter as nobody got a free day off this go-around.

Brian Dyson, when grilled by the press about June sales figures for the new Coke, replied in his wonderfully precise English accent that they were up in places and down in places but that overall the company sensed in the consumer what he delicately termed "a withdrawal of enthusiasm"—a sort of "Coke-itus Interruptus," if you will.

There were a lot of lessons learned in the bargain. Coke learned that the science of market research can take a pulse but miss a heartbeat. America learned that the voice of the Little Man can still be heard in the panelled walls of Corporate America. Pepsi learned that you can't make a better cola with sour grapes. And the whole world learned that original Coke, now a "Classic," was, as they say in West Georgia, a hard dog to keep under the porch.

*July 1985*

# GREASING YOUR CHOPS IN STYLE

Dining out is in and dining in is out. Fast food, feminism, frozen dinners and frantic lifestyles have all combined to make home cooking as out-of-date as curb feelers, merry widows and kissing with your mouth closed.

With families all over the country hopping from one new "in" spot to the next, it occurred to me that closer attention should be given to the basic manners of eating out. I mean, sure, we all know that unless your dining spot has little Tabasco bottles on the table with green peppers in them or a chrome toothpick dispenser at the cash register, you are not supposed to put your cigarette out in the mashed potatoes or soak your uppers in the water glass. But there are more subtle tips for the unwary diner in the area of manners and, from time to time, my friends and admirers, aware of my history as a frequenter of fine food establishments dating back to the mid-1950s and Bowdon, Georgia's famous Chez Spatula, will come to my chambers seeking counsel as to how they might avoid the more egregious dining gaffes that seem forever to beset the less worldly diner.

Though it is true that I am now considered to be to *haute cuisine* what Jackie Collins is to classical literature, there was a time when I was not nearly so sophisticated.

A flush still colors my face from rugged brow to flaccid wattles when I recall a college graduation banquet for members of the Honor Society where I, the very epitome of West Georgia worldliness, startled students and professors alike at my table when, in mid-sentence, I paused to pick up with my fingers and eat a butterball that had just been placed on my bread plate. How one could have lived twenty-one years and still not recognize a butterball I cannot say, but the moment I bit into it, there flashed across my brain in marquee-size letters—BUTTERBALL! My effort at recovery by observing to the stunned and queasy professor sitting next to me, "Now, that's a good butterball," only added to the general embarrassment.

It may well be that a lack of sophistication in dining is a congenital defect, for, little more than two decades later, I suggested to my sixteen-year-old son that he take his prom date to one of our city's most elegant restaurants, and the outcome was again less than stellar. Before setting him loose, I was careful to brief him on all the intricacies of restaurant manners, such as proper utensils and tipping and warned him not to follow his usual practice of putting his napkin in his collar and wrapping his arm around his plate like a dog guarding a bone. I truly thought I had covered all possibilities and was somewhat surprised to find him at the breakfast table the following morning looking glum in the extreme.

"How did your dinner date go?" I inquired.

"Not well," he muttered.

When pressed further he revealed the problem: "When the waiter came to our table he said, 'I'm John and I'll be your waiter this evening' and I got up and said, 'Hi, I'm Josh,' and shook his hand."

I tried to tell him that this show of democracy was not altogether bad and, while a bit unsophisticated, was not a sign of bad manners at all.

"Maybe so," he said morosely, "but then I introduced him to my date."

In my mind, this serves to illustrate that even in the most cosmopolitan of families, a diner not properly schooled in the etiquette of eating out can wind up with egg (or worse) on his face. I take these matters up in considerable detail in my upcoming opus *Eating Out Etiquette or Don't Floss Until After the Demitasse Cups Have Been Removed*, now in the hands of my publisher, Simon and Lipschutz (New York, Philadelphia and Austell). However, because of some nettlesome litigation filed by Miss Manners, who claims that some of the best tips in my book were simply plagiarized and warmed over bits from some of her nattering nonsense, publication will likely be delayed for some time. Thus, I think it useful to share a few of the mannerly morsels in advance:

(1) To begin at the beginning, the male diner should not loutishly forge into the dining room ahead of his female companion when the pair is being shown to their table. Moreover, if he and his companion have stopped at the bar for a libation prior to dining, the gentleman should not allow the lady to carry her own drink to the table. Rather, unless he wants her to look like Sadie Thompson scouting for sailors, he should allow her to follow the maitre d' to the table and should

himself carry their drinks to the table or ask the bartender (on the off chance he is able to regain his attention after paying the check) to send the potables along.

(2) Unless the dining establishment is a rib shack or a truck stop, a gentleman diner will wear a jacket and a necktie, or, at a minimum, some sort of garment that will permit neighboring diners to enjoy their meal without having to gaze at an expanse of chest hair that would convince them that a family of flying squirrels is mating in his pectorals. This goes double for hairy males in tank tops.

(3) Sophisticated diners should remember that tasting wine is a delicate and quiet business and should not cause those at adjacent tables to conclude that one is a test pilot for Lavoris.

(4) Makeup is not to be applied at the table by women diners, or, if we are talking about the growing number of *chez gay* restaurants found in rejuvenating sections of most major cities, by any diners.

(5) One should not draw attention to one's party by tipping the waiter off that it is Uncle Raymond's birthday. There is nothing so dreary to other diners as having a gaggle of waiters skip in, bunch up and shrilly sing "Happy Birthday" while one of their simpering number stands by with a sparkler sticking out of his cupcake.

(6) Do not keep your table any longer than it takes your party to eat and have coffee and after-dinner drinks. Remember there are other diners waiting for the table. In fact, they are waiting in the bar, getting drunk and mad, comparing you and your loutish group to Japanese holdouts on Okinawa, and threatening to come in and pummel all of you within an inch of your senses.

(7) Bear in mind that you are fooling no one when you ask for a "doggy bag." Know too that there is no sadder or sillier

sight in the world than that of a well-dressed diner scuttling through a posh restaurant clutching a greasy brown bag.

There are, of course, many, many more, but this brief starter set will certainly raise your sensibilities as you flit from spot to spot enjoying *nouvelle cuisine* (French for "tastes bland") pending the release of my more comprehensive effort. In the meantime, happy trails and *bon appetit*!

August 1985

# A SHOOTOUT WITH
# A TEXAS OXYMORON

Is it any wonder that from Rabun Gap to Tybee Light the mention of *Journal-Constitution* causes a Pavlovian response of "them lying Atlanta newapapers?" How can it be otherwise when the publisher of both papers goes public with an extraordinary claim that "barbecue beef" is a redundancy rather than an oxymoron?

David Easterly, publisher of the *Atlanta Journal-Constitution* and a known Texan, in last Sunday's combined edition, caused the publication of a rank heresy he had previously uttered to the effect that "Barbecue is beef."

The slender logic behind his premise seemed to be that this was so because many years back some Texans had corrupted a well-established culinary tradition and actually barbecued cows. Well, of course, they did. You can't ride a horse and steal a pig at the same time.

I see absolutely no need to rekindle regional prejudices by pointing out that Texas was, after all, settled by renegade Georgians who generally left this jurisdiction fleeing some sort of legal process, that it has always been thought of as the Byzantium of Bluster, or that for some time even after it was finally admitted to the Union, its standard form of currency was buffalo chips, but I do think that in the interest of setting the record straight and restoring what shred of credibility the Atlanta newspapers had before this calumny was uttered, I ought to bring some light and logic where ignorance and chaos have been allowed to reign.

Just because someone cooks something the way barbecue is cooked and covers it with a barbecue-type sauce, this doesn't mean that it is genuine barbecue. In Texas there are even people who barbecue baby goats. (Just wait till the crowd that has been jumping up and down about Eskimos and baby seals find out about that.) Certainly Mr. Easterly wouldn't claim that this leads him to the conclusion that barbecue is baby goat, for goodness sake.

It is a well-known fact that Texans do not read very much—their lips are said to tire very quickly—but there is documentary evidence that this matter was well settled many years ago. The English poet Alexander Pope wrote, "Send me, gods, a whole hog *barbecued.*" While Texans persist in the belief that recorded history began with the calamitous defeat of Sam Houston at the Alamo (just one more example of their rigid and unyielding perversity), I would point out to Mr. Easterly that Pope (1688-1744) was around long before mesquite was developed as the Lone Star State's chief money crop.

# THE SASS MENAGERIE

In this context, it may be more than just coincidence that Pope also coined the maxim "A *little learning* is a dang'rous thing" and, in the same work ("Essay on Criticism"), wrote "Be not the first by whom the new are tried,/Nor yet the last to lay the old aside" (obviously a poetic allusion to yahoos who would seek to replace the traditional pork with the upstart beef). And, still later in "An Essay on Man," he wrote, "And, spite of Pride in erring Reason's spite,/One truth is clear, *Whatever is, is right."* I think this says it all.

Even in the Bible (I think it is Deuteronomy, but I'm not completely sure) there is the admonition to "Beware of false prophets from the west, who will draw nigh unto you and bear false witness about barbecue and cows and stuff."

I see no need to prolong Mr. Easterly's embarrassment by driving further nails of logic and learning into the casket wherein his spurious argument now reposes, but, in the interest of preserving the remnants of the *Journal-Constitution's* tattered image, I would urge that in the future, if he persists in going about outside the state of Texas and ordering barbecue beef in public, he wear a *yarmulke.* Then folks could at least think he was motivated out of religious conviction rather than ignorance.

In closing, I would simply say that if barbecue isn't pork then, to borrow the words of one of our great contemporary American poets (I think it was either Robert Frost or Clyde McPhatter), "Eggs ain't poultry, grits ain't groceries and Mona Lisa was a man."

*September 1985*

# THE NIGHT LIFE
# AIN'T NO GOOD LIFE,
# BUT IT'S MY LIFE

In my ever-shrinking circle of friends (people tend to become more and more distant the better they know my wife), I am generally thought of as something of a sophisticate. Even on school nights I can be found dressed to the nines and eating out with my angular and haughty spouse.

Yet, in spite of my madcap ways, I and my friends are forever puzzled as to why my name is never mentioned in Ron Hudspeth's gossip column, as in "Dilettante columnist and *bon vivant* Bob Steed and wizened wife seen dining at (fill in name of some restaurant)."

"Maybe," my wife suggested querulously, "it's because Ron Hudspeth doesn't eat at Morrison's all that much. Maybe, too," she continued with what I thought was the trace of an edge in her voice, "Ron Hudspeth stays out later than nine o'clock at night."

"Maybe," I shot back fiercely, "it's because there is no such person as Ron Hudspeth. Maybe the rumor, long hushed up by the Atlanta newspapers, that Celestine Sibley gets roaring drunk every weekend in Sweet Apple and knocks out five columns at a time over his name is true. (In truth, as far as I know, no one has ever seen Ron Hudspeth in person and the photograph that appears with his column has never looked real to me. I've always suspected it was done by a police sketch artist.)

My suspicions about Hudspeth aside, I will confess that I was somewhat stunned by my wife's implication that my style of night maneuver was not as trendy as it might be, and I quietly resolved to dive deeper into the dark underbelly of Atlanta's after-hours scene.

Some weeks later as we were leaving Morrison's (I recommend the Thursday-night special featuring all the salmon patties you can eat for $1.19), I flicked the ash from my English Oval and, smoke drifting from one nostril, casually suggested to my wife that we "pop by 'Pat and Barbara's' for a nightcap." I had read in the entertainment section that this fashionable DeFoors Ferry nightery was the hottest new opening in town.

Identifying myself at the door as a columnist for the *Atlanta Constitution*, I discreetly palmed a dollar bill to the burly doorkeeper who greeted us and was immediately ushered to a choice table well away from the noisy stage and very convenient to the men's room.

My after-hours instincts, as always, proved impeccable. It is impossible to imagine a group more lively and entertaining than the Pat and Barbara chorale. They are more fun than a carload of whoopee cushions.

The leader of this motley group is Pat Horrine Motley who sings, plays two guitars (though not at the same time) and was formerly a member of either the New Kingston Trio or the Ink

**21**

Spots, I forget which one they said.

The other half of the eponymous ensemble is the lively and absolutely luscious Barbara King, who first broke into show business some years back at Six Flags Over Georgia, where she was working as a ride. Ms. King is a quick-witted, funny and formidable stage presence. Moreover, she is—let's say it—sexy. But in sort of a homespun way—picture Sally Field on steroids. Beyond that, she has more moves than Dominique Wilkins and can play kazoo and sing up a storm.

Grizzled bass player Curt Walters (whom many will remember from the love scene in *Deliverance*) is Gabby Hayes reincarnate one moment and can cause a meltdown in your soul the next with his nuclear version of "You Are the Wind Beneath My Wings."

Young David Gould looks like a defrocked CPA but can play a harmonica so sweet and pure that it would make Mickey Raphael of Willie Nelson's band twitch in unrestrained and galvanic envy. He has riffs so soulful they would bring tears to a bank loan officer's eyes.

From their tasteful and restrained opening number ("Take Your Tongue Out of My Mouth 'Cause I'm Kissing You Goodbye") to their heart-wrenching close ("Please Come to Smyrna in the Springtime"), they were absolutely unique, entertaining, funny and fantastic.

After their first set, the sultry and smoky Ms. King, like a heat-seeking missile, found her way to my table. She introduced herself with a warm hand clasp and eyes filled with promises of more to come and cooed, "They say you're a columnist for the *Constitution*. Maybe you could write us up."

"Well," I stammered, "I'm not really. I mean I am, but I'm not regular. I mean, well, maybe I *could* get you a mention in Ron Hudspeth."

"Oh," she brightened, "do you know Celestine Sibley?"

*September 1985*

**22**

# DO THE NAME RUBY BEGONIA MEAN ANYTHING TO YA?

Television critic John Carman may well have blundered across that invisible but treacherous line that separates "preaching" from "meddling." In a recent column, he made so bold as to suggest that the venerable TV series *Amos 'n' Andy* be freed from its solitary confinement in the vaults of the Columbia Broadcasting System.

His heretical notion is that the program, having lingered in this unofficial limbo for so long, is now ripe for freedom and could be sold into syndication without giving wholesale offense to the phalanx of folks who have traditionally jumped up to be its detractors.

As a longtime fan of the series, I admired Carman's courage if not his judgement and was further pleased when that venerated *wunderkind* of American letters, Lewis M. Grizzard (b. Moreland, 1946) came out of the closet a few days later and admitted in public that he had been watching videotapes of the program for some time. Next thing you know, we'll find out he's got a Jane Fonda workout tape tucked away in his collection.

Carman, much in the manner of one whistling while walking through the graveyard, also evoked the names of comedian George Kirby and the Rev. Jesse Jackson in support of his suggestion that *Amos 'n' Andy* be granted amnesty. But in the background I could hear the roar of knees beginning to jerk, and I freely predict those traditional foes who always seem to pop up on this question will simply have a fit. Carman must learn that rubbing logic up against emotion serves only to make matters worse.

Reasonable folks can disagree on subjects even as trivial as this, and I think we have to stipulate that offensiveness is largely in the eye of the beholder. My guess is that *Amos 'n' Andy*, having been a punching bag for so many years, will be once again denied parole by those who have always railed against it. I predict that once the furor has reached its fulsome fury, CBS would as soon invite Ted Turner over for a spend-the-night party as free *Amos 'n' Andy*.

I agree with Carman that the show was historically important, well-written, beautifully acted and very funny in the bargain. Tim Moore as the picaresque and cunning King-fish was, in my mind, a comic genius, and keeping his talent in the can for nineteen years seems a genuine crime and a ringing irony.

Carman also might have added the name of Sammy Davis, Jr., as one who appears to have found the program great good fun. For years, his public utterances have been filled with catch phrases from the show, and I have always thought that a good possible format for reproducing it would be to style it as a "Comedy Classic Series," which, of course, it is, with Davis as its narrator.

To those who will continue to pillory the program as being an unsavory stereotype, I would suggest that they could better vent their spleen on other comic examples in the contemporary marketplace. Richard Pryor, who I think is also a comic genius, does more material in dialect in a minute than Amos Jones did in a year. Moreover, every other word in a Pryor routine is either scatological or his favorite relentlessly uttered and incestuously oedipal two-word expletive. Yet, curiously, he doesn't provoke the reflexive outrage that seems relentlessly to follow *Amos 'n' Andy.*

Russell Baker recently observed that "The land is swarming with people willing to spend their lives being offended, whether the offender is offensive or not." While Carman and Grizzard are to be commended for exposing their editorial flanks to the ever-lurking and inevitable fangs, they must learn that having sown the wind they will reap the whirlwind.

And, for those who are bound to resent having logic injected into an otherwise thoroughly emotional issue, I'll apologize in advance by borrowing just one of many of the Kingfish's more memorable malapropisms and humbly ask that they "'Scuse me for protruding."

*July 1985*

# TURN YOUR HEAD
# AND COIF

Ever anxious to avoid even a trace of sexism in my thoughtful and well-reasoned prose, I am careful to root out any suggestion, however subtle, that might be read as supporting the heretical notion that there exist any differences between the male and female of the species.

Notwithstanding this firmly held conviction, my senses will occasionally be jolted by some aberrant fact or circumstance which, by sheer reflex I'm sure, will cause me to revert to biases I formerly harbored before reaching a state of grace through the assiduous study of the words and works of Alan

# THE SASS MENAGERIE

Alda.

By way of recent example, I was reminded of a prejudice I used to hold to the effect that women seem to have a pathological preoccupation with their hair that is not shared with the same unwholesome fervor by males.

This dangerous flashback was occasioned when I read a human interest story in the morning paper about an elderly Atlanta legal secretary who had retired to Roopville, Georgia, and was living with two cats in a disabled '73 Pontiac so that her thirty-seven dogs could enjoy her house trailer. Neighbors, concerned by indications that the lady was severely neglecting her own well-being in favor of providing food and comfort to her four-legged friends, had called in the appropriate authorities to assess the situation.

The investigators discovered that she had indeed sacrificed her quarters, her Social Security checks and all manner of personal comforts and necessities so that this Malthusian mob of mutts would be comfortably sustained.

Happily, an "animal welfare group" interested in the upkeep of stray dogs was located, and cash was promised to ameliorate the woman's plight. This is where my flashback flashed. After saying that the extra money would permit her to feed and fence her dogs and reclaim her quarters, she concluded with this amazing statement: "And I'd like to do something about my hair."

It gives one pause that a woman who has chosen a life of self-sacrifice so extreme as to live in the hulk of a busted Pontiac would still, at the prospect of sunnier times, think about her long-neglected coif.

I have long observed that the mood of my sinewy spouse was adversely affected with every change in the length or hue of her hair which, at one unhappy point, was switching colors with the frequency of a chameleon scurrying around a Christmas tree. I also recalled that when I pressed my older daughter, Georgia, to consider Tulane as a college that she might seek to attend, she summarily dismissed the idea by saying, "Are you kidding? That humidity in New Orleans would make my hair fall."

The unhealthy and sexist thought became so strong that I could overcome it only by watching some videotapes of old Phil Donahue shows, and, I'm happy to report, reason finally began to regain control.

The reasoned answer is that both women *and* men are equally obsessive about their hair, and you need go no farther than your nearest TV to verify this fact. John Forsyth of *Dynasty* fame has gone to a rinse so purple that his head looks like a grape with a part in it. Jim Bakker of the PTL Club turned silky blond overnight in a miracle more likely wrought by Miss Clairol than divine intervention. Evangelist Ernest Angley, not trusting his own formidable healing powers to restore his missing hair, appears to have covered his noggin with a toupee that looks like a bad piece of Astroturf.

It was a great relief to be back in harmony with the mainstream of modern feminist thought. As an interesting aside, I might point out that my uncle, George Lee Steed, was one of Roopville's most innovative mayors. He fulfilled a campaign promise to double the city's revenue simply by installing a second parking meter. Later, as a solution to Roopville's traffic congestion, he ordered that all streets be made one-way. Over three-fourths of the community found themselves stranded in nearby Franklin, Georgia, before it was discovered that Roopville had only one street.

The former mayor could not be reached for comment about the story involving the lady and her dogs.

*October 1985*

# TURKEYS I
# HAVE KNOWN

The Editors
*Peachtree Papers*
Atlanta, Georgia

Dear Ladies:

Your question regarding "turkeys I have known" takes me back to November of 1958 and stirs memories of the first Thanksgiving dinner prepared by my new bride of three months. I was in Mercer Law School and operating on a budget so tight that very little money was available for groceries. By happy coincidence, my wife was from a family so poor that the only pet they had been able to afford for her was a medium-sized turkey which, by then, was quite old and could no longer run in the fields with her or jump and catch Frisbees in its mouth. Although torn between her love for the pet and her desire to please me and a law school professor whom I had invited for dinner in the hope that it would bolster my sagging grade point average, she said we *would* have turkey that Thanksgiving. On Thanksgiving evening, as promised, she brought to the table the richly browned, glistening and steaming turkey and asked me to carve. "What did you stuff it with?" I asked, ending my inquiry with a smile and a preposition.

"I didn't have to stuff it," she said. "It wasn't hollow."

I quickly put the carving knife aside and treated everyone to dinner at the Pig 'n' Whistle, then one of Macon's finest drive-in restaurants.

I should, in fairness, point out that my wife disagrees with me every time I recount this story. She says there was no law professor and she never had a pet turkey but that she does remember that I took her to the Pig 'n' Whistle for a Dutch-treat Thanksgiving dinner. Friends who have heard both versions and knew neither of us back then tend to agree with her account, pointing out that she was, after all, a home economics graduate from Wesleyan College and even now her legendary recipe for instant coffee ("Put one level teaspoon of Maxim in a cup, add boiling water, stir briskly. Serves one.") is a northwest Atlanta favorite and has appeared in many cookbooks.

With warmest regards, I am

Easily aroused,

Robert L. Steed

*November 1985*

# "O WAD SOME POWER THE GIFTIE GIE US"

I hate to sound like Andy Rooney (for that matter, I even hate for Andy Rooney to sound like Andy Rooney), but I've concluded that buying good Christmas gifts for daddies is tougher than getting discount auto insurance for Hosea Williams.

In the first place, the entire holiday season, it seems to me, is patterned along the lines of a drill for sinking ships, i.e., women and children first. I went through a half-dozen hefty Christmas catalogs in last Sunday's paper and came up with only three presents that seemed even remotely appropriate for the daddy market—a Pollenex foot bath, a "smoke grabber" ashtray and a blood pressure machine. Actually, I wouldn't care for any of those items separately, but I think if they got them all together in one piece of hardware, they'd really have a nice consolation prize for some of those daytime game shows.

As a public service to daddies everywhere, I thought it might be useful if I took a few moments from my busy holiday schedule to issue something in the nature of a Christmas Shoppers Advisory, giving examples of some definite downers in the Christmastime pantheon of presents for Papa:

(1) First on the list would be chocolate-covered cherries. These loathesome confections seem literally to spring out of the woodwork at Christmastime and represent, I believe, a blatant attempt by candy makers to foist off something that is otherwise inedible because it might be bought at Christmastime since it is red and covered with chocolate. As far as I know, the primary use for cherries is to decorate those large, fruity drinks ordered by people who really don't drink all that much. I understand cherries are sometimes used to make pies up north, but then those people eat rutabagas and raw meat and don't know what you are talking about when you ask for sweet milk.

(2) Any of those shaving lotions that cost over five dollars a bottle and make you smell like the Gabor sisters.

(3) Body jewelry. There's nothing sadder than a flabby old man in an open-front shirt with a gold neck chain hanging about his flaccid wattles. In that same connection, I think that legislation should be enacted making it a crime for any male to wear a ring on his little finger unless he is playing an accordian at the time.

(4) A "PC" which, I am told, stands for personal computer. I don't need a personal computer. I have a cheap pocket calculator that has seven keys I can't identify a function for. While we are talking about PCs, I think the Varsity ought to

sue all those computer people for violating their trademark. As anyone knows, PC means "plain chocolate." Always has.

(5) Electric hair dryers for men. Recent studies at the California Institute for the Sexually Suspect have revealed that prolonged use of electric hair dryers will cause men to walk funny and, in some extreme cases, even to break into a skip. Worse yet, they can do some funny stuff to your hair. I once used my daughter's hair dryer and wound up looking like fight promoter Don King.

(6) Anything that runs on batteries.

(7) Any of that Jim Palmer-type underwear. That stuff looks all right on Jim Palmer, but daddies need a shoehorn to get into it and then look like a hundred pounds of suet in a fifty-pound bag.

(8) Those "Fruit of the Month" offers. I am always afraid that, if I got one of those, someone would show up at my door early in the year and say "Hi, I'm Keith, I'll be your fruit for the month of January."

(9) Pajamas. I suppose that there are grown men who actually wear pajamas, but I think it can be proved that most of them are in public institutions such as veterans' hospitals, nursing homes or the State Home for Old Pipe-Smokers. These people also wear bathrobes and bedroom slippers. Again, most of this stuff is sold and worn up north, but then they also eat rutabagas and raw meat and don't know what you are talking about when you ask for sweet milk.

I know that this is the season to be jolly, and I truly hate to be negative in such an otherwise happy time. But if these thoughts cause just one father to be spared a bottle of Halston cologne, then my efforts will not have been vain.

*Joyeux Noel!*

*December 1985*

# COWED, FLUMMOXED
# AND BAFFLED

Some have suggested that it is more than mere coincidence that the Georgia General Assembly and Ringling Brothers Barnum & Bailey Circus both come to Atlanta at the same time every year. As for me, I see nothing either sinister or redundant about it but do think our legislators ought to spend less time clowning around and more time addressing the truly important issues of the day.

Of course, they must undertake their annual grappling with the ever-cosmic issues of legislative salaries, pensions and skywalks between the state office buildings and the state

Capitol, but I suggest there is other equally urgent business that, for the past few sessions, has simply gone untended.

Widely known as a deep thinker with a long and incisive political view (my essay written while still a senior in high school on "What Harold Stassen Means to Me" won top honors in the Carroll County American Legion competition in 1954 and was, for a time, seriously considered for publication in the *Reader's Digest*), I am often sought out by newly elected members of the General Assembly who, when confronted with the formidable presence of Speaker Tom Murphy or the intimidating mountain wiles of Lieutenant Governor Zell Miller, find themselves cowed, flummoxed and baffled (not to be confused with a small firm of CPAs in Doraville by the same name).

With the firm conviction that it is every citizen's duty to participate in the governmental process, I thought it might be useful to lawmakers, both old and new, if I briefly certified a few legislative needs which, in my considered judgment, are of the highest priority:

(1) Of course, something must be done about academic standards for college athletes. I am close to a number of college coaches in the state and, while they prefer not to be publicly identified, I think it is safe to say that they would all welcome a crackdown in this regard. Of course, they don't want the legislators to overreact to the current crisis. As one of them said to me, "I think if a student dresses out at between 250 and 295 pounds, can bench-press a Honda, and runs the forty in under five seconds, you ought not to ask any more of him than to keep the crayon colors inside the lines."

(2) I think legislation ought to be passed outlawing these little stoplights that people are putting in the back windows of their automobiles. If the driver purchased the automobile with the light already in it, a warning ticket should be issued. If the driver actually had the light installed, he should be given a citation and made to attend Tacky School.

(3) I think Waffle Houses should be limited to every other interstate off-ramp.

(4) A law should be passed denying the right to distribute within the state's borders any national magazine that comes with those obnoxious little "blowout" cards that scatter in all directions when the magazine is opened.

(5) Tammy Faye Bakker and Sally Struthers should not be allowed to appear on two television channels at the same time. If something isn't done soon, these lachrymose ladies will have the entire populace in a state of deep depression.

(6) More money should be put into the Governor's budget for speech lessons. While our Chief Executive seems to be steadily gaining ground on those pesky verb tenses, I continue to be extremely anxious that during one of his speeches some English teacher is going to jump on the stage and attempt a citizen's arrest.

(7) No adult male should be allowed to wear gold neck chains unless he can prove he (i) is Italian, (ii) has current employment singing in a cocktail lounge, and (iii) knows all three verses to "Feelings."

(8) Joggers who continue to clog and clutter the public roads and thoroughfares should be required to register themselves and wear little license tags.

(9) There should be an absolute prohibition against those relentless radio commercials featuring what sounds to be a pair of senior citizens flushed out of a nursing home up north somewhere who are forever chirping "Your Anchor Banker, *he* understands. Your Anchor Banker, *she* understands."

(10) Laws should be enacted standardizing the spelling of the name of Cathy. It can be either "Cathy," "Cathie," "Kathy" or "Kathie," but this permissiveness that now exists is sapping America's moral strength and making us look indecisive abroad.

## THE SASS MENAGERIE

(11) A bill must be enacted banning the sale, distribution or consumption of nachos in movie houses. Previous legislative attempts to stop this growing, un-American and thoroughly disgusting practice have been thwarted repeatedly by crafty veteran legislator Tom Buck of Columbus, who, as a private attorney, regularly represents some of the most powerful nacho growers in southwest Georgia.

I know there will be some reactionary members of the legislature who would prefer that I keep my suggestions to myself rather than causing undue pressure on the legislative process by publicly airing proposals brimming with basic common sense. However, as one truly great American said (I think it was either Hoss Cartwright or Renee Richards), a man's got to do what he thinks is right.

*February 1986*

# TV COPS JUST
# AREN'T ARRESTING

I have stood around long enough while public opinion of law enforcement officers has plummeted in a steady spiral (actually, I was sitting down a good part of the time and even stretched out and dozed off occasionally when it got dark). Clearly, however, the moment has come for those of us who mold and shape the nation's thinking to stop looking the other way and to begin speaking out on this deplorable state of affairs.

While criminologists, sociologists, and other deep thinkers ranging from Phil Donahue to Merv Griffin wring their hands and wonder aloud as to why the criminal element hold the law enforcement community in such complete disdain, I am convinced that the answer lies no further than the nearest Sylvania Superset.

I believe it was either Alexis de Tocqueville, René Descartes or Willard Scott who first observed that "Television is proof in living color that the worst to come is already here."

The sad fact is that television shapes all of our perceptions, and the current state of policemen on television is calculated to make them objects of either pity or derision.

Consider, if you will, that the hottest police story currently on the airwaves is a rainbow-hued pastiche called *Miami Vice*, the heroes of which are two guys named Crockett and Tubbs, who dart about in fushia sport coats with the sleeves rolled up. These guys do little more than drive around in convertibles in a blur of rock music and change clothes more often than Linda Evans does. When they get a suspect in for questioning, you're afraid that, when the interrogation-room door closes, instead of getting out the rubber hose, they'll try to fix his hair or tickle him silly. The producers tried to macho up the pretty one with a three-day stubble of beard, but it served only to make him look like a wino interior decorator.

How can we expect this generation of TV addicts to respect the police establishment when these two bozos are leaping around like a pair of pastel gazelles in a rock video?

When I think back to my TV days, I remember folks like William Gargan, Reed Hadley of *Racquet Squad*, Lee Marvin of the *M Squad* and Broderick Crawford on *Highway Patrol*. Now there was a redoubtable image of a police officer — Broderick Crawford complete with beer belly, felt hat and a thousand-word vocabulary. That's my idea of a cop.

Now we have the even more improbable police show involving the psychodramas of two — get this — female street cops. I'm speaking, of course, of the thoroughly unbelievable Chris Cagney and Mary Beth Lacey, who are forever police-crouching around stiff-armed with their pistols in both hands as they try to look menacing without mussing their hair. As if the concept in general didn't do enough damage to our credibility gag reflex, in recent episodes the one who looks like Ernest Borgnine continues to kick in doors and terrify the forces of evil even though she is heavy with child. I can remember in the old days when in police jargon "bust" meant an arrest, not having a detective's water break during hot pursuit.

Whatever happened to the TV detectives like Steve McQueen, Burt Reynolds and Robert Stack? They've been replaced by amoral role models like Daniel J. Travanti, who on *Hill Street Blues* plays a police captain who is so righteous and straight that during working hours he squeaks but, through the first couple of seasons, wound up every episode in a double bed with the sloe-eyed, smoky public defender, nuzzling like two overheated spaniels. Although he finally made her an honest woman, what can the youth of America be thinking? I can tell you it causes towering outrage in one of my generation who grew up avidly reading Dick Tracy in the newspapers for his "Tips to Junior Crime Stoppers" ("In case of kidnapping, be sure to examine the victim for suspicious fingerprints on or about his body"). You never caught Broderick Crawford bouncing around on the Beautyrest with some hussy at the end of a *Highway Patrol* episode.

The saddest part of all this is the fact that while these disco-dicks and females who look like they ought to be in the intensive-care ward at some European health spa are getting all the good TV detective jobs, former television policemen like Efrem Zimbalist, Jr. (*The FBI Story*) have been reduced to doing cameo appearances on the *PTL Club* with Jim and Tammy Fay.

I'm just glad that *Dragnet*'s Jack Webb passed on to that big precinct station in the sky before all of this came about, or we might be seeing him hosting *Family Feud* or hawking Slim

## THE SASS MENAGERIE

Whitman albums on Channel 17. *"Sic transit gloria,* Friday."
Support your local police. Watch reruns.

*March 1986*

# HOLD THE
# PHONE

In March of 1982 I struck a blow for good telephone manners, the reverberations from which are still ringing in the ears of people throughout the civilized world and even in parts of L.A. (Lower Alabama).

My now famous monograph on the odious and uncivilized "telephone call-waiting device" which, while its owner is talking to one person, emits an obnoxious sound (somewhat like a rat barking) to alert both parties to the conversation that yet a third party is calling, has been cited by scientific and sociological journals as the definitive word on the subject and is thought to be responsible for shaming many Type-A house-wives into abandoning the churlish device altogether for the more traditional and well-mannered busy signal. Others, who are too compulsive to give up this rude and bitter fruit from the technological tree, are now aware that most callers consider the rat bark an ill-mannered and gratuitous affront and at least have the good taste to be embarrassed when the interruption occurs — "Oh, I'm so sorry. This could be an emergency. You know my husband has a spastic colon."

So well received were my trenchant and forthright obser-vations on this bit of rudeness that my publishers, Simon & Lipschutz (New York, Philadelphia and Austell), urged me to steal a march on Miss Manners and rush into print with a comprehensive exposition on the subject of telephone etiquette in the workplace. The book was scheduled for publication in early spring but has been delayed as my barristers do battle with a battery of pettifoggers in the employ of Dr. Ruth Westheimer, who is claiming prior rights to my proposed title — *Reach Out and Touch Someone.*

In the meantime, in the interest of civil behavior in the office (and in the hope that a pre-publication tease might help flog the sales of this dubious literary enterprise), I have succumbed to growing pressures and agreed to reveal some of the problems and solutions relative to this unhappy state of affairs.

With business calls, as in the case of domestic calls to one with a rat-bark device, a simple busy signal would be a marvelous alternative to falling into the clutch of an officious and overprotective secretary. When returning a telephone call, I am piqued in the extreme when the caller's secretary, having been informed that I am returning his call, asks, in a tone mixed with self-importance and exasperation, "Will Mr. Slip-shod know what this call is in reference to?"

In such cases I will often reply, "Perhaps not. This is Inspector Throckmorton of the Good Grammar League, and we're checking on a report that Slipshod's secretary ends her sentences with prepositions."

Just as vexing is the secretary who, after I have placed the call in the first instance and asked for her boss, priggishly inquires, "Will Mr. Allison know what this call is about?"

I have several stock replies for this bit of impertinence:

(1) "Based on my experience with Mr. Allison, he won't know what the call is about even after we're through speaking."

(2) "Just tell him I want to know what he's going to do about my wife."

(3) "This is Dr. Garcia from the clinic. Please tell him that his tests are back and that I need to speak to him right away. And, Miss, I don't even know you, but I'd suggest that you not shake hands with him or touch anything he has handled until we clear this business up."

(4) "Yes, tell him that we've retouched the nude photos he made of himself in the booth at K-Mart, but the stretch marks still show."

Usually any of these tested rejoinders are sufficient to shake the secretary from her torpor and produce her nervous employer, who was likely doing nothing more important in the first place than his daily nose calisthenics.

Another bit of telephone insolence that causes me to firmly set my jaw (at least as firmly as my ample wattles will permit) is answering my phone and having someone's secretary say, "Will you hold for Mr. Weatherwax?"

My standard response is "I don't know, would Mr. Weatherwax hold for me?" Or, "No, but as Weatherwax apparently wants to speak to me, I'll ask my secretary if she would be good enough to hold until he can get his big fat butt to the telephone." Implicit in all of this business is a power struggle as to just who is the more important—the caller or the person being called.

I realize, of course, that some people are so important that they cannot and should not be expected to place their own telephone calls. Obviously, President Reagan can't place his own calls (some Democrats claim that he hasn't been able to do so since the crank telephone was phased out), but I find that most of the people who have their secretaries place their calls are suffering from nothing more serious than bad manners and self-importance.

My upcoming literary opus will also address many other habits and traits in this connection, such as operators who answer the phone with "Please hold" and then leave you suspended like Mohammed's coffin between heaven and earth while they doubtless chat on with their chums about who sired someone's child on *As the World Turns*; canny callers who return your call during lunchtime with the hope that they won't have to speak to you but will get credit for making the effort; secretaries who ask you to leave your number and *then* go for a pencil; secretaries who demand one's name, rank and serial number before giving a direct response to a simple query as to whether their boss is in; and business offices who put you on hold in a telephonic limbo of recorded music or, worse yet, a radio talk show.

My secretary, who appeared to be in a strange humor after typing this preview, suggested tersely that I might also include a chapter on bosses who are always telling their secretaries to "Find out who he is"; "Find out what he wants"; "Tell him I'm in conference"; or "Get Allison on the phone." She's probably overheard some of this from other bosses in our office.

*March 1986*

**45**

# I HATE TO RAIN ON
# YOUR INANE PARADE

Is it just me, or are there others out there in the real world who have an overwhelming suspicion that the questions allegedly written in to those celebrity information columns in the newspapers are not really sent in at random from live people but are manufactured in-house? I don't want to sound overly skeptical, but I certainly have my doubts.

A good example of the type feature that causes my ears to elevate and shift forward and my brow to form a jaundiced pucker is "Personality Parade," a regular Sunday offering in the magazine section presenting questions of cosmic concern, which purportedly have been troubling our country's deep thinkers from coast to coast.

For instance, the first compelling question in the last such feature I read was, "The other night I watched on TV an old movie, *National Velvet*, starring Elizabeth Taylor, Mickey Rooney and Angela Lansbury. How many times has each of these former kid stars been married?" Well, I was breathless until I could read the answer to this stimulating question. It was, "Elizabeth Taylor has been married seven times, Angela Lansbury twice and Mickey Rooney eight times—for a grand total of seventeen marriages." (And we wonder why Mickey's complexion looks so bad these days; it's nothing more than rice marks.)

If some grown person with a full set of teeth actually sent in such a question, shouldn't a Presidential Commission be created to look into the fact that there are people out there who are watching *National Velvet* and wondering how many times the cast have been married? For all we know, these same people could also be voting or operating motor vehicles.

Another question in the same issue begged for more information on Charles Kuralt of CBS News. Those who have seen Charles Kuralt on CBS News will fully appreciate what I mean when I say that this question is a textbook example of what is called "morbid curiosity." As might be imagined, its propounder did have the good judgment to remain anonymous by identifying himself (or "himself or herself" as we of the consciousness-heightened set like to say) as "M.E.G., of Rensselaer, NY."

Another titillated soul from Allentown, Pennsylvania, was tracking down a rumor that Princess Caroline of Monaco was planning to ditch her young husband for Argentine tennis star Guillermo Vilas after giving birth to her second child. I know that many of us have been particularly concerned about this possibility, and I was very relieved when "Patrice B." was assured that "There's little or no chance" Caroline would dump her hubby (whose job description was "Italian heir") for the tennis star. World money markets reacted to the news positively by continuing to devalue the dollar against Monaco's currency which is, I believe, poker chips.

I hate to sound cynical about all this, but I really have difficulty believing there are adult human beings out there in America who really care about this nonsense to the point that they are moved to sit down and write in such questions. My guess is that they're all composed in-house by some ex-Valley Girl whose brain, for various pathological or chemical reasons, is starved for oxygen.

As an exercise in support of my premise, I set out to conjure up some "Qs and As" of my own, and in the space of just a few minutes came up with what I believe to be a fairly typical collection of the inane inquiries that bubble up in these frothy offerings. For example:

**Q.** Is there any truth to the rumor that Andy Rooney and Mickey Rooney are related? — B.M.W., Munich, Germany

**A.** Andy Rooney is Mickey Rooney's oldest child. His mother is Ethel Barrymore, who was Mickey's first wife.

**Q.** Is it true that there have actually been cases of animal brains having been successfully transplanted to human beings? — Mary Shelley, Crumpet on the Thymus, England

**A.** In late 1975, a team of surgeons successfully transplanted the brain of a cocker spaniel into the body of Sylvester Stallone. For obvious reasons, information on this radical procedure has been effectively suppressed for over ten years by top-ranking officials of the American Kennel Club.

**Q.** Is Phil Donahue's hair really that color? — Danny Thomas, Beirut, NJ

**A.** Those close to Mr. Donahue say that the color is not natural but results from the fact that Donahue regularly "freebases" with "White Mink" by Miss Clairol.

**Q.** If Muammer Khadafy is so damn smart, how come he's still a colonel? — R. R., Washington, DC

**A.** Muammar Khadafy is recognized even by his severest critics as a "brilliant military tactician" but, according to secret Libyan government records, has repeatedly failed to gain promotion because of "poor grades on the written portion of the Generals' Test, owing to a profound learning disability and repeated incidents of dirty brass during inspections."

Lest anyone take this hypothesis of mine too lightly, I would remind them that it was I who first broke the story that there was no such person as Ron Hudspeth. I know that's not his picture they use with his column. Inside sources tell me it is a photo of the lad who formerly appeared on cans of Dutch Boy house paint and who is now almost sixty-five years old and in a detoxification center in New Jersey being treated for sustained turpentine sniffing.

*April 1986*

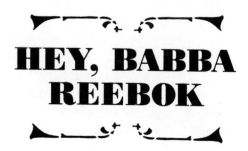

# HEY, BABBA REEBOK

There is something afoot in downtown Atlanta and other major metropolitan areas that needs some serious looking into and, when I say "afoot," that's just exactly what I mean.

I don't know if the increased radiation in the atmosphere is resulting in some low-level brain damage or if the feminist movement is just manifesting itself in yet another perverse and bizarre fashion protest, but increasing numbers of females have been spotted on city streets dressed to the nines but wearing those grisly running shoes that look like orthopedic possums with laces.

I've always been a fool for high heels but at a tasteful height, of course. I don't favor those ultra-high numbers like Tammy Faye wears on the *PTL Club,* which make the wearers look like out-of-control downhill racers. Nor do I care for those tawdry backless platform jobs that were in vogue a few years back. You know, the ones that seemed to cry out "Hi, Sailor. In town long?"

No, just give me a basic pair of two-inch heels with no gnarled toes poking out the front, and I'm quite content and convinced that I. Miller is in his heaven and all is right with the world.

But now, great Ferragamo! Legions of ladies are schlepping up and down Wall Street, Peachtree Street and every other prime business artery in America in their secretarial finery or professional female two-piece suits with little Dale Evans string ties, bottomed out with these hideously deformed clodhoppers that look like canvas room dividers.

Like so many other loathesome trends, this abomination apparently began in New York City. There, at least, it has some meager logical basis in that the working women shod in these Manhattan mutations do, in fact, often walk twenty or thirty blocks to their place of employ. Their Atlanta counterparts generally have to navigate only two or three blocks from the MARTA station nearest their office.

There is a serious lack of logic in this business. Why would these women want to look their worst when they're being seen by the most people they'll be exposed to all day? It causes a flashback in my mind to my teenage years in Bowdon, Georgia, when swarms of our dirt-road debs would come to town on a crowded Saturday afternoon looking like the road show of *Grapes of Wrath* and wearing so many curlers in their heads that they were picking up Mexican radio stations. All of this just so their hair would look good for some adenoidal adolescent in the back seat of a '52 Chevy at the drive-in movie that night.

This murky business, coupled with a random and unexpected surge of blood to my brain, brought to mind a plethora of vexing questions: Why are these women doing this? If their regular shoes are all that uncomfortable, why not wear these canvas clubfeet all day long, and, if comfort is the answer, will they soon start coming to work in their bathrobes? What if the male population starts affecting these buffoonish appendages and begins bringing their tassel loafers to work in briefcases? Do these pitiful pumps serve some deep unmet need, or will they be just another faddish, female fashion affectation like droopy ballet leg warmers; wearing towels like sarongs at the swimming pool; lip gloss that makes the wearer look like she's just finished off a big glass of Quaker State; grocery shopping in jogging suits; the mandatory sunglasses perched blindly on the top of the head; or, worst of all, those textured hose that look like some exotic leg disease?

I'm sure this too shall pass, but in the meantime we'll just have to endure yet another fashion fad with all the charm, allure and sex appeal of an advanced case of athlete's foot.

*May 1986*

# METHODIST DEMILITARIZED ZONE

One morning recently as I sat at the breakfast table attempting to jump-start my heart with a steaming mug of my wife's famous home-brewed instant coffee, I heard gurgling sounds of disapproval from her side of the morning paper.

She was, it turned out, reacting as violently as her customary morning torpor would permit, to a news story revealing that a National Hymnal Revision Committee of the United Methodist Church has uttered a solemn recommendation that "Onward Christian Soldiers" be dropped from the church hymnal because, according to the press account, "of its militaristic overtones." Herself a militant Methodist since her days as a young guerrilla in the Bowdon MYF, my leathery bride began to vent her spleen with remarkable vigor given the fact that she is generally unable to formulate complete sentences until around 11:00 A.M. or later.

As a licensed Baptist, I have never considered the church of John Wesley to be a bastion of orthodoxy, but I was forced on this occasion to side with my sinewy spouse and observe that this gratuitous heresy was a bit extreme even for the doctrinally mercurial Methodists.

The only good news in the press account was that an army of fifteen hundred delegates (roughly two battalions) to the South Georgia Methodist Conference in Macon rose up in righteous indignation at the proposal by the National Committee and smote it hip and thigh.

Still, one wonders why grown people, many of them presumably high-school graduates, would think to form a National Hymnal Revision Committee in the first place. Certainly there must be other endeavors which, if not less useless, are at least less mischievous and divisive.

According to the news story, the headquarters (a fairly militaristic term itself) of the Committee had been deluged with angry letters from flared-nostriled Methodists who were up in arms over the proposal. The article said that a 1985 church survey found that 69.4 percent of Methodists favored keeping "Onward Christian Soldiers" in the hymnal. One would like to think that the other 30.6 percent thought the suggestion to delete it so wimpy in the first place that they didn't even bother to reply.

Thumbing through my vexed mate's Cokesbury Hymnal (copyright 1938—Lord knows what purges it may have suffered since then), I wondered at what other old favorites would be demobilized by the persistently pacifist addle-pates on the Revision Committee. Military metaphor seems to abound in so many of the traditional songs—"A Mighty Fortress Is Our

God," "Marching with the Heroes," "Stand Up, Stand Up for Jesus (Ye soldiers of the cross . . . The trumpet call obey . . . Put on the gospel armor, etc.)" and, on page 229, that old jingoistic "Star-Spangled Banner" which, one assumes, will just have to go.

In the spirit of ending denominational discord, I would offer a compromise (the mother's milk of any committee conclusion) and suggest the songs found offensive by the Hymnal Revision Committee be left in the hymnal but that any congregation caught singing them be required to give equal time to opposing sensibilities by going to page 259 of the 1938 Cokesbury Hymnal and singing three choruses of "Down by the River-side": "Ain't goin' t' study war no more, ain't goin' t' study war no more, ain't goin' t' study war no more."

In the alternative, the Methodists could simply put aside their bickering, love everybody and stop quarrelling with one another. Like the Baptists, for example.

*May 1986*

# REEBOK
# REDUX

I recently shared with my readers (a sturdy but steadily dwindling band) my impression that many females had been victimized by a grisly fashion trend that features dressing them up in their work-a-day best but causes them to put on nasty-looking running shoes while going back and forth to their jobs. It was my lighthearted hope that by gently calling attention to this ugly fad, many ladies would come to their senses and abandon the practice, shifting into the less unsightly but equally comfortable low-heeled sandals, flats or (and this may date me as a child of the fifties) ballet slippers.

In ringing affirmation of the eternal verity of the maxim that "No good deed goes unpunished," many of the women readers took the effort in just the wrong way and accused me of being insensitive and mean-spirited in the extreme. (One comely young woman in our office, however, did accost me in the elevator and rapturously declared that she had seen the light after reading my column and had taken her Reeboks to the nearest landfill. I was swept by a rush of surprise and accomplishment that must approximate just how Ernest Angley feels when he has restored the hearing of one of his parishioners with a pop in the forehead. The fact that the young woman wasn't offended by the article is probably attributable to the fact that she is from Tallapoosa, Georgia, and lacks the acute sensibilities of the militant feminists in metropolitan areas.)

More typical of the hostile reaction to the gentle and well-intended piece was a presentation ceremony in my chambers staged by my soon-to-be-ex-paralegal, Rebecca Chandler, who interrupted a meeting to present me with a pair of high heels along with a challenge that I wear them to the nearest MARTA station and back. I declined on purely aesthetic grounds. The shoes were red three-inch heels with air vents all around the top causing them to resemble the hood of a 1954 Buick Roadmaster.

Moreover, a number of women posted hostile letters claiming that by singling out this particular fad, I had committed some sexist slur. Why, they insisted, did I not publicly deplore male fashion aberrations?

Why indeed! My record in this regard is absolutely unimpeachable. One has only to study the body of my work to see that I have been an outspoken tower of courage in heaping invective on abominable male fashion trends. To cite but a few specific examples:

(1) It was none other than Robert L. Steed who, in August

of 1980, first revealed that early onset brain damage was being caused in many males by the use of gale-force blow hair dryers.

(2) It was Robert L. Steed who in April of 1981 spoke out against males who cause nausea in public restaurants by dining in those shiny open-front shirts exposing chests that look as though the diner has just coughed up a fur ball or is permitting a group of chinchillas to nest in his pectorals.

(3) It was Robert L. Steed who as early as June of 1982 first spoke out against those noisome male colognes that cause the wearer to smell like someone who has just been criminally assaulted by a gang of Avon ladies.

(4) And, also in the area of air pollution, it is well documented that I was one of the first to speak out against the resurgence of cigar smoking, pointing out that the cigar was originally invented as a breath freshener for people who eat dead birds.

(5) I believe I can say without fear of contradiction that I was one of the earliest commentators to speak out against gold neck chains hanging about the droopy wattles of middle-aged American males and even suggested legislation prohibiting any males from wearing rings on their little fingers unless they were licensed gigolos or had a permit to play an accordion.

(6) In a rare but piercingly honest moment of self-examination, I spoke out against dress shirts of the type that I often affect — those colored jobs with the white collars — pointing out that they are foolish looking. (Even I don't wear them when I return to my hometown of Bowdon, Georgia, as the rustics there persist in their conviction that they are "factory seconds.")

(7) Throughout my career, I have been an outspoken critic of males who swirl a few remaining strands of hair back and forth over their bald pates in a fashion that ultimately resembles a potholder made by a child at summer camp.

# THE SASS MENAGERIE

In sum, I think my record is clean and clear in terms of even-handed assessment of odious fashion trends of both sexes. I speak out without fear or favor and bitterly resent any implication that my observations in this regard have any anti-feminist tinge.

I maintain, however, that those women who wear clunky running shoes back and forth to the MARTA stations really do look like dorks.

*June 1986*

# HONOR AND OBEY? THAT'LL BE THE DAY

I don't believe I can recall a recent time when the newspapers and airwaves have been so literally awash with good news. There are the thrill-a-minute Goodwill Games in Moscow, and, of course, we're all excited that Jim and Tammy Faye Bakker, the high priest and priestess of the *PTL Club,* have recently completed their big water slide at Six Flags Over Heaven. But for me the biggest and brightest news in recent weeks was that Sarah Ferguson publicly revealed that she will include "love, honor *and obey"* in her nuptial vows when she ties the Windsor knot with Prince Andrew next month.

## THE SASS MENAGERIE

A return to traditional values of that magnitude certainly warms the cockles of my heart (I was diagnosed as having heart cockles in my early forties, but, except for an inability to perform any strenuous exercise or household chores of any kind, I am able to lead a full and normal life).

Newspaper dispatches, which are being cranked out on a daily basis to keep up with the voracious appetite of those of us in the New World eager for every detail of these royal doings, further reveal that Princess Diana selected an alternative rite when jumping the broomstick with Prince Charles, allowing Diana to drop the "obey." One assumes that references to spousal obedience were included when Queen Elizabeth exchanged vows with Prince Philip. I don't know that to be the case, but every time I see the two of them together he looks as though she has just taken him by the ear and said, "Clasp your hands behind your back, look interested and follow me."

I am fascinated by these interesting tidbits being fed to the masses by the royal flacks. Did you know that Sarah and Andrew are the first royal couple following the Industrial Revolution who have never received an electric appliance as a wedding gift? They have, however, received six sofas confirming, I assume, that royalty is expected to do more sitting than cooking. I wish I had known this earlier. I would have been glad to send them an electric wok instead of the gift I finally chose—a wooden hamburger press bearing the Steed coat of arms (a ruptured capon on a field of fleur-de-lis).

My grizzled wife, a commoner to the core, does not share my enthusiasm for these fascinating inside glimpses of royal life, callously lumping them with the Goodwill Games and Jim and Tammy Faye. I attribute this difference of opinion to an unfortunate incident that took place almost forty years ago.

Since I played King Cyril of Happyland to rave reviews in the 1948 Bowdon Grammar School production of the operetta *Sunny*, I have always felt a deep and abiding affinity for royalty. In the raging grip of puberty, my rendition of the operetta's most memorable tune, "I Can't Laugh Anymore," was literally a show stopper. Owing to the raging hormones, my voice could span three octaves, often on the same note. I was told that our musical director, Miss Leila Arrington, later referred to my performance by saying, "I never heard anything like it."

On the other hand, the performance of my wife, cast in a minor supporting role as the Gentle Southwind, was not nearly so well received. I think the pans of her performance came about because she had difficulty remembering her lines and because, even though she was costumed in a see-through, harem-type outfit, her unsympathetic parents refused to let their hairy twelve-year-old shave her legs. In any case, it has seemed to me that, from the late 1940s on, her attitude toward royalty has been undeniably flip and callow.

Lest Prince Andrew find himself in the grip of some ingenuous premarital trance and take the promise of obedience in the wedding vows as having some real significance, I think I probably ought to drop him a line when we mail the hamburger press to let him know that he is going to be riding for a real fall after the wedding day. "Love, honor and obey" in the wedding ceremony ranks right along with describing women as the "weaker sex." It's just an expression.

Prince Andrew needs to know that "obey" in a wedding vow is just another quaint but meaningless term. It ranks right up there with "plighting your troth." I recently had dinner with a lady from Macon who said she had "plighted her troth" three times and still didn't know what she had done. As a veteran of almost three decades in the stormy path of the gale force Gentle Southwind, I can certainly understand the "plight" part of it. In time, so will Prince Andrew.

*July 1986*

# IN THE LAND OF THE EASILY AROUSED

In the much ado about next-to-nothing category, I would like to place in nomination the recently released (though *escaped* may be a better choice of verbs) Meese Report.

To a chorus of yawns, the Attorney General's Commission on Pornography released the carnal cat from its cellophane bag saying that, "Obscene publications which depict child pornography and violent and degrading behavior toward women are socially harmful." Talk about apostles of the obvious.

The AG's porn posse was stacked from the start with a majority of literary vigilantes whose biases in this regard were

already well established, and their split-decision report, though at odds with a previous and better financed government effort in 1970, contained nothing very surprising. The tedious and predictable ramblings of this Anti-Smut SWAT Squad would probably have passed without notice but for the fact that prior to the release of the Report, the Commission fired off a threatening letter to major convenience stores and pharmacy chains warning them (presumably under cover of the United States Department of Justice) that they had been identified as being "involved in the sale or distribution of pornography" because they stocked magazines deemed unacceptable to the Commission, including *Playboy* and *Penthouse*.

A couple of the chains, notably 7-Eleven, buckled under the implied government threat and quit peddling those publications. This caused a morally outraged *Playboy* to sue Meese and the Commission and, predictably, raised the hackles on civil libertarians from sea to shining sea. (For those who have never actually seen a raised hackle on a civil libertarian, I can tell you it is *not* a pretty sight.) That great American philosopher David Letterman tried to put matters in some perspective by cogently asking how 7-Eleven could justify banning *Playboy* as "obscene" while still continuing to sell Slurpees.

Aside from questions of the First Amendment, due process, black lists and gratuitous government intimidation, the thing that most convinces one that the Commission must have been watching *Leave It to Beaver* reruns throughout the sexual revolution is the notion in their threatening letter that the bland and voluptuously vapid *Playboy* is obscene.

The pneumatic, silicone-supplemented, empty-headed, air-brushed and blemishless beauties that adorn *Playboy*'s pages from month to month are about as erotic as merry widows or elastic stockings. *Playboy*'s founder and self-styled Sybarite, Hugh Hefner, has been locked for three decades in a sexual time warp and only recently conceded that his corseted

Playboy Club bunnies were a little dated in an era in which even doughnut shops in Florida were going topless.

Similarly, by any contemporary measure, even *Penthouse* is tame in this day and time. In keeping with the somewhat sleazy style of its founder, Bob Guccione (who, in his open-front, shiny shirts with yards of gold chains draped around his neck, always reminds me of a Las Vegas men's room attendant), the subjects of *Penthouse* spreads are a tad more earthy than their more wholesome *Playboy* counterparts. However, they are light years from obscene by any standard definition. But, as my old masseur used to say, "There's the rub," because there is no standard definition of obscene. It is all in the steamy loins of the beholder.

In this regard, I think the collective arousal level of the Commission must have been much like that of the pathologically prurient soul who was arrested for some deviant behavior and was being administered a Rorschach test by a battery of psychiatrists after having been certified to them as hopelessly depraved.

As the psychiatrists revealed the series of ink blots to him, he would respond with incredibly graphic descriptions of the lewd and obscene images they provoked in his mind's eye, each description being more disgusting than the one before.

Finally, one of the doctors interrupted the test and told the patient that he was the most thoroughgoing and hopeless degenerate he had ever encountered in his thirty years as a psychiatrist.

The angry patient screamed, "I'm a degenerate? I'm a degenerate! You guys are the ones with all the dirty pictures!"

*August 1986*

# TEENSPEAK TERRORS

As I lounged lumplike and leaden by the steaming pool of a club in the northwest quadrant of the city, the babble of nonstop teenage patter drifted through the torpid haze in an unending and ungrammatical stream. Treading the thin white line that separates heat stroke from hallucination, I wondered vaguely why America's youth — even the inmates of some of the city's most expensive schools — is so stunningly inarticulate.

Could it be the effect of long-term brain-baking by years of powerful TV rays? Is there some toxic agent in Clearasil that somehow seeps into the teenage cortex and stunts that portion responsible for comprehensible speech? Do decibel-deafening rock music and electric hair dryers forever numb or fricassee the faculties required for coherent communication?

Two northside debs in my immediate earshot came upon one another after an apparent absence of a day or so and, after obligatory shrieks of recognition and delight at this serendipitous reunion, lapsed into an argot that bordered on the untranslatable.

I have long deplored and, on occasion, publicly decried the perverse tendency of today's youngsters to confuse the verb *to go* with the verb *to say*, but after a few minutes of involuntary eavesdropping on these two bubble-heads, my mind was literally screaming for even a trace of grammatical utterance.

"So she goes like, 'What do you mean Madonna got her hair cut?' and I go like, 'Really, I saw her in a video and she's like trashed that grody old bra and has, like, really short hair.'"

Another phenomenon in the current speech pattern of the pimply people is a persistent and grating habit of responding to any declarative sentence with the word *really*, as in:

**Deb I:** "Where have you been?"
**Deb II:** "Like, we visited my grandparents in Newark."
**Deb I:** "Really."

The response is not intended to convey incredulity (though reacting to the above example some might wonder that one would voluntarily confess to having kinfolks in New Jersey), nor is it an exclamation of approval (the word *neat* is used in those situations). Rather, it is simply a completely neutral verbal reflex indicating nothing more than "I understand."

In response to my minor fulmination on this particular trend, my nineteen-year-old daughter, Nona, offered that it was nothing more than the modern-day equivalent of "Is that so?" or "You don't say?" When I huffily observed that those phrases were never used in the south but were employed almost exclusively in the vapid reaches of the midwest, my leathery spouse, who was lounging nearby in the manner of a languid lizard on a hot rock, dreamily revealed her humble origins by pointing out that the southern equivalent of "Really" was "Do tell."

Sensing that my outcries were falling on deaf and indifferent ears, I plunged back into my steamy reverie and wondered if prior to the time the Roman Empire slipped beneath the surface with a great sucking sound there had been a distant early warning in the form of a total breakdown in the speech patterns of their teenagers, e.g.:

"Like, Flavius, those games are like fixed. I mean, like, those lions are just pretending to eat those Christians."

"Really."

*August 1986*

# JUST SEND MY BODY HOME ON A FREIGHT TRAIN

Country music is in a schizophrenic state. Singers like Crystal Gayle (formerly Loretta Lynn's sister) have gone to singing songs that are more pop than country. Crystal's latest is an old 1950s Johnny Ray effort—"Cry"—and in it her pronunciation sounds like she came out of a finishing school instead of a coal mine.

However, in all of this confusion, there is still discovered once in a blue moon a set of adenoids so flawlessly formed and capable of a twang so exquisitely resonant that their owner is certain to catapult to country-and-western stardom. It was my great pleasure to discover such a classic set of nasal appendages one recent evening while grudgingly pub crawling with my leathery spouse and some of her lowbrow country music friends.

She and one of her more unusual looking renegade colleagues, Lawyer Ragsdale (picture a shifty-eyed presence who looks like a cross between Muammar Khadafy and Gabby Hayes), led a pack of us to Miss Kitty's, a suburban *boite* that features rising country stars and Texas terpsichore on a dance floor the size of a small landing strip.

The featured attraction for the evening was to be a young singer named Randy Travis. While we awaited the appearance of young Travis, I was beguiled at the panoply of taxpayers who acted out their cowboy fantasies by hooting and hopping about in western shirts and jeans, ten-gallon hats festooned with exotic feathers and tooled boots, all combined in costumes that would make Lash LaRue look like a CPA. Equally amazing was to see them all stomping about with Buzz Berkley precision doing the Texas Two-step, the Sweetheart Schottische and the Cotton-eyed Joe.

Having grown up in a family whose musical tastes were exclusively classical (my parents are thought to own one of the largest collections of Rosemary Clooney albums in West Georgia), I was not familiar with Randy Travis and, in truth, was not terribly keen to add any facts about him to my already overtaxed data bank. As luck would have it, I stumbled into a doctor friend who, after assaying our party and wondering aloud as to how I had fallen in with such low company, volunteered with obvious pride that he was personal physician to young Travis. "He is an extraordinary young man," he said, "doesn't smoke, drink or do drugs." Then, leaning closer, he added conspiratorially, "And he has less than 5 percent body fat."

"Well," I ventured, "I can put him on a program to help with that body fat."

## ROBERT L. STEED

Brushing aside my offer, the doctor began rapturously to detail just what a rapidly rising star young Travis was in the country music galaxy, only to be interrupted when the featured performer came on stage to pandemoniac applause. His modest manner and bearing offered no hint of what proved to be the clearest, cleanest, most appealing country sounds I have ever heard. While his style and sound are totally his own, there are pleasant echoes of Ernest Tubb, George Jones and Hank Williams, Sr. His choice of material was outstanding as well. Eschewing the lewd lyrics that currently abound in country music, he stuck to the classic trail with poetic images of lost love, freight trains, going home, etc. — each selection ringing with the double and triple negatives so warmly cherished by country singers:

Just send my body home on a freight train
And don't worry none that I don't go first class.
Send my body home on a freight train,
So everyone can see me when I pass.
Don't worry none about no fancy funeral
'Cause it don't matter how they lay me down.
Just see they bury me out by Mama's apple tree
And send my body back to my hometown.

Fiercely blinking back the tears, I thought, "Percy Bysshe Shelley — eat your heart out."

As is always the case with great discovery, I was eager to share the glad tidings with those not among the cognoscenti, so, the following day during a golf match with that hirsute man of letters, Lewis Grizzard, I said to him as he furtively poked his ball to a higher spot in the rough, "I've just heard a great new country singer — Randy Travis." The ever-querulous Grizzard snapped, "You're right on top of things. I guess you heard that Nixon resigned. It was in all the papers."

"You mean you've already heard about Travis?"

**74**

"'On the Other Hand,' '1982,' 'Digging Up Bones,'" Grizzard ticked off as he stroked his beard and kicked his ball onto the fairway with a flair that would have made Kevin Butler twitch in unrestrained envy. (As an aside, it might be interesting to note that based on Grizzard's facial hair, many meteorologists are predicting a very severe winter.)

On the off-chance that there are still those who have not heard Randy Travis, I commend him in warm and unqualified terms. As that great American philosopher Brother Dave Gardner used to say, "He's flat got it."

Travis's best selections can be found on his album *Storms of Life*, and my favorite is one called "Then You Started Messing with My Mind," which features—of all things—a clarinet solo. It sounds as though Benny Goodman had been shanghaied by the Sons of the Pioneers.

And, remember, you heard it here first.

*October 1986*

# DEEP IN THE
# HEART OF COBB

While pundits and politicians throughout the civilized world do dreadful and dubious battle over whether there are "two Georgias," a more urgent conundrum lies at our very doorstep. I'm referring, of course, to the "two Cobb County" controversy.

There are denizens of our sister county to the north residing in the posh Republican reaches of Cobb communities with exotic names such as Vinings, Smyrna and East Marietta who would have the outside world to understand that all of Cobb is but one unending and elegant expanse of worldliness and sophistication, as characterized by the glittering Galleria, the lavish homes that cling serenely to the lofty banks of the stately Chattahoochee, and the lush polo fields near the Atlanta Country Club, upon which the creme of Marietta society gambol and cavort (many of them on horseback).

Yet others — perhaps cynical MARTA officials vexed and embittered over continued rejection of mass transit by the ever-xenophobic Cobb Countians — hint darkly that there is another side to Cobb, pointing to the lanky yeomen who cruise about in strap undershirts and billed caps, affect long, stringy side-burns and drive gun-racked pickup trucks perched on grossly oversized tires designed to support heavy earth-moving equip-ment. They quote statistics from the federal government to the effect that there are more tattoos per capita in Cobb County than in any other jurisdiction in the United States with the possible exception of Demopolis, Alabama.

For reasons that I am unable to explain, I seem to have been drawn into this controversy and am often the object of long-distance inquiry on the subject from sociologists, political scientists and talk-show hosts throughout the United States and several provinces in Canada who are following the "two Cobb" question with single-minded determination. Scarcely a week passes that I do not receive an urgent call from some breathless investigator eager to probe deeper into the question of whether there are, in fact, two distinct Cobb counties. There is some talk in television circles that Geraldo Rivera is consid-ering doing a special on the subject as a logical follow-up to his thrilling and thought-provoking live coverage of the opening of Al Capone's safe in that demolished Chicago hotel.

I suspect that I was thrust into the eye of this sociological storm when I, while making a major policy speech before the Snellville Kiwanis Club, unwittingly characterized Cobb County as "the point on the compass where sophisticated suburbia collides head-on with Hee-Haw." In my remarks, which were calculated merely to allay the growing sense of inferiority that has engulfed the citizens of those counties that

lie near Cobb, who are becoming increasingly intimidated by the swelling *savoire-faire* and almost European worldliness of Cobb County, I pointed out that there remain pockets in Cobb that continue to mirror the rest of Georgia. Specifically, I revealed that in late 1985 a group of anthropologists had discovered, living in the woods, near South Cobb County's Austell, Georgia, a small tribe of people who still worshiped the Big Chicken.

"Are there, then," you are doubtless asking, "two Cobb Counties?" I prefer to make no answer to a question of such cosmic consequence for fear of giving offense to those in all parts of Cobb who harbor such strong feelings on the subject, specifically my brother-in-law, Wayne Preston, a prominent resident of that jurisdiction, who for years has been searching for some pretext, however remote, to keep from paying me back some money I loaned him in 1968.

However, I am convinced that the question is one of real importance and worthy of greater study. For if Cobb County is, as many scholars suspect, merely a microcosm of the state of Georgia, then the answer to the nettlesome "two Georgia" question that has so long bedeviled and divided deep thinkers here and abroad may well lie in a closer study of Cobb, its citizens and culture.

As Alfred Lord Tennyson (who incidentally was born in 1809 on what is now the site of the K-Mart in Marietta) so aptly observed in his "Flower in the Crannied Wall":


Flower in the crannied wall,
I pluck you out of the crannies,
I hold you here, root and all, in my hand,
Little flower—but if I could understand
What you are, root and all, and all in all,
I should know what God and man is.

## ROBERT L. STEED

I think what Al is saying here, as it related to the "two Georgias" controversy, is that if we can ever understand Cobb County, we may well have broken the code.

*October 1986*

# MERCER: NO. 9
# WITH A BULLET

At the breakfast table one morning recently while attempting to galvanize my gastric juices with a glass of Donald Duck canned fruit juice, put before me by the somnolent former home-ec major across the table from me, I was bowled over by a dispatch in the morning paper revealing that my alma mater, Mercer University, had been designated by *Playboy* magazine as No. 9 in its annual survey of Top 40 Party Colleges. With a center of gravity that has tended to get larger and lower with advancing years, I am generally regarded as one who is difficult to bowl over, but this bit of news was simply too much even for my growing equilibrium.

My mind reeled with troubled thought as to how things could have changed so since my undergraduate days when Mercer was a cloister of rectitude, right-thinking and scholarship.

As is well-known in better educational circles, Mercer University was founded in 1835 by the Reverend Jesse Mercer as a refuge for students who were too poor to go to Emory and too proud to go to the University of Georgia. From its earliest days it was a paradigm of piety and erudition. Matters had not changed much by 1954, when my parents took me to Bean's Drugstore, which served as the bus station for Bowdon, Georgia, and put me on a southbound Greyhound with nothing more than a shoebox of fried chicken, eighty-five cents in change, a rubber sheet and a lapel sign saying, "Put this boy off in Macon."

Looking back I can say without reservation that in 1954 Mercer had about as much chance of getting on anyone's Top Party College list as Dr. Ruth has of getting named Dean of Women at Oral Roberts University.

The attitude of the school's administration towards any activity beyond study and character development was nothing short of reactionary. By way of example, coeds were permitted to wear shorts to gym classes, but while they were traversing the campus or otherwise in public view, they were required to wear a raincoat lest their young bodies excite lascivious thought on the part of leering law students. (The advantage this rule gave the Wesleyan College students during the bathing-suit portion of the Miss Macon Contest was inestimable.)

The 1954 Student Handbook, in a rule that would now be thought sexist, provided that "No female student shall be permitted to smoke in public unless, of course, she is actually on fire."

Stricter still was the rigid and almost pathological prohibition against dancing on campus. To make it sound more insidious, the administration characterized it as "mixed dancing," and any such carnal activity was absolutely proscribed. As editor-in-chief of the hard-hitting, world-famous *Mercer Cluster* (the journalistic incubator for fourth-estate luminaries such as Bert Struby, Jack Tarver and Reg Murphy, the last of whom left Atlanta under cover of darkness in the trunk of an automobile), I began what was to become a lifetime affliction of intemperate railing in print when I injected myself into the eye of a theological hurricane by suggesting that, contrary to the then-prevailing view of the Baptist hierarchy, there was no solid clinical data to support their notion that the box step was contributing to the decline of western civilization or that it led inevitably to that pernicious activity described in Deuteronomy as "begetting" (at least it never had in my case).

Such rank apostasy invariably provoked paroxysms of consternation in the ranks of the administration officials and among the ministerial students who swarmed the campus in great numbers, and, once again, I would find myself number one on the Mercer Prayer List maintained from week to week by those good and pious scholars. It's worth noting in the context of partying that those students' idea of a good time was to go down to the city jail and sing hymns to the inmates. The inmates were finally successful in getting the practice enjoined as a violation of their Constitutional rights against cruel and unusual punishment.

That in a mere thirty years the institution could have drifted so far from its charted moral course will (taking into account that Mercer still is, to borrow Ferrol Sams's marvelously apt expression, "Baptist to the bone") surely cause in some of the righteous ranks feelings of dread and loathing and provoke some mild moaning, gnashing of teeth and renting of garments (Mercerians are notorious for renting garments, particularly tuxedos, which only a few of them can afford to own). But as for this aging rebel who fulminated so fulsomely and ineffectively against the rigid puritanism of the fifties, my honest reaction to the *Playboy* news was "Where did we go right?"

*December 1986*

# PEANUT BUTTER BRAINS

For some time now I have become increasingly convinced that the most pernicious threat to our western civilization lies not in the Red Menace, pit bulls, school prayer, the environmentally hostile "greenhouse effect" or even the deadly grammatical patterns of our youngsters. Rather, it is the persistent and poisonous mind pollutant pumped directly and relentlessly into our homes in the form of cable television.

While other less concerned citizens choose to ignore this threat and follow their own trivial pursuits, I, in sporadic fits of patriotic fervor, dive into my humpback leather couch at intervals and, like Jacques Cousteau, probe the murky electronic depths of cable television, surfacing occasionally to sound an alarum that doubtless will go unnoticed and unappreciated. But, then, everyone thought Geraldo Rivera was crazy too.

I am something of a virtuoso on the remote control keyboard. With deft, lightning-like strokes, I can do a fly pattern through sixty-plus channels of pap and drivel (not to be confused with the large Atlanta advertising firm of the same name) and thus keep a jaundiced eye on all the troublesome activity infesting our electronic subconscious. I had hoped that my life's companion, the former Linda McElroy of Bowdon, Georgia, would dedicate herself to this vigil as well. However, my condition that I exclusively maintain the remote control device, coupled with congenital torpor and an overwhelming lack of intellectual curiosity on her part, made joint action impossible. I truly believe the woman would watch one program for four or five minutes at a stretch if I didn't take matters into my own hands. She has so thoroughly poisoned the minds of my own family members against me in this regard that even our family dog begins to twitch uncontrollably when I turn on the television.

Probably the most distressing recent development on cable television is the advent of TV fishing. There are actually people in our society who are watching two bozos in a bateau bobbing about in some god-forsaken backwater *fishing*. The dialogue goes something like this:

**Play-by-play angler:** "Boy, howdy, that's a big 'un!"
**Color angler:** "That *is* a big 'un."

Whereupon they reel in a carp for a cameo appearance, hoist it for the camera and then, for reasons I have not been able to fathom, release it. What chance does our civilization have for the long haul when we know that there are grown people who, presumably, are licensed to drive automobiles and are doubtless producing children, who sit for long intervals watching other people catch fish and turn them loose day after day?

Another ominous development is telemarketing. One fascinating program emanating from, where else, California, features a beefy pitchman who, at first blush, seems to be auctioning off a variety of remaindered goods to a crowd that looks as though they would gather to see a root canal. The crowd keeps bidding the merchandise higher and higher, which causes a skinny stooge to the right of the auctioneer to get so excited that he begins to whirl on his axis like a demented dervish approaching a state of huckster rhapsody.

Finally, when the dreck merchandise has been bid up to a point where the auctioneer dare not risk exciting his sidekick further, he does not, as one might suspect, sell it to the highest bidder. No, he announces that the unbelievable merchandise (brass hatracks, zircon-encrusted gold unisex neck chains, horse statues with clocks in their stomachs and the like) will not sell for sixty-five dollars as bid but will go for $19.95 to all those who will "get up and call in now." Further to encourage sluggish TV shoppers, he then begins to squeal out the card numbers of the lucky bidders in the rented audience while banks of telephone operators gird their loins to take orders called in by hapless bargain hunters from sea to shining sea.

But this is just one of the ways to effect a transfer of funds to TV performers from the eager and easily mulcted souls who so avidly follow their electronic antics. Witness the continued fiscal success of the swarm of televangelists that *Time* featured in a cover story on the burgeoning phenomenon. My personal pick from the preachers now swarming the airwaves is the Bakkers, Jim and Tammy Faye, who are forever bobbing about in a sea of fiscal crisis, but, just when they have convinced you that their ship is about to slip beneath the surface with a great sucking sound, the faithful respond with shekels enough to float it even higher. Tammy Faye seems to apply her makeup with a trowel (I live in fear that someday she will be found slumped in a doorway, overdosed on a bad batch of Maybelline), and the Reverend Jim, with the love offerings of the faithful, has just completed what may well be the largest water slide in Christendom. All summer long he appeared on the airwaves looking like a forlorn chipmunk in a yellow hard hat importuning his TV parishioners to send in more money to complete the water slide. I had visions of one of his flock sliding down the towering monster, flying off its unfinished edge, swooshing and landing with a deadly thump in Beulah Land. Happily, the project was completed during the summer, and the Bakkers now offer, in addition to traditional spiritual succor, a kind of Six Flags Over Heaven in Fort Mill, South Carolina. The connection between organized religion and water sports seems, to me, tenuous at best, but this is, I suspect, a matter best addressed by philosophers and theologians.

Rapid clicking of the remote control buttons reveals a phantasmagoria of faces that includes Regis Philbin, Dr. Ruth, the ever-lachrymose Sally Struthers, a meat house of wrestlers shouting imprecations into the camera and a cooking show featuring a bagged-out Creole in red suspenders who keeps saying, "I gar-roon-*tee*."

This stuff, I'm sure, is turning our brains into that old-fashioned peanut butter with the oil slick on top, and my guess is that there is some central sinister force behind it all.

Stay tuned.

*January 1987*

# COUCH POTATOES UNITE!

My friend of many years, the corpulent counselor Tom Watson Brown, shares my aversion to the compulsive physical fitness mania that now has so many trendy citizens firmly in its sweaty grasp. With a secret glee equaled only by that of a very old person who has just learned that a slightly younger contemporary has crossed Jordan's stormy banks, Brown will often send me clippings of articles debunking the salutary properties of jogging, aerobics or other rigorous forms of self-improvement.

His day is made if he can come across an obscure article to

the effect that jogging cauliflowers one's brain, ravages the joints or flattens the arches. Just as felicitous to him is news that some runner arrogantly claiming a portion of the city streets has been impaled on the hood ornament of a Dodge Dart.

While I lack the girth of Tom Watson Brown (he was the first Harvard Law School graduate ever to be fitted for curb feelers), I am noted for a growing tendency to "bunch up" when I sit down. Thus, it is natural enough that he keeps me on his mailing list for these macabre alerts that physical fitness isn't all it's cracked up to be.

I know it gave him considerable pain recently to send me a dispatch from the University of California-Berkeley "Wellness Letter" (January 1987) to the effect that sustained watching of football on television could be hazardous to your health. The "Wellness Letter" reported the case of an otherwise healthy forty-year-old man who was brought to Massachusetts General Hospital with a pulmonary embolus in the arteries leading to the lungs. The sports fan had gotten up on New Year's Day and repaired immediately to his sofa to watch three consecutive bowl games. He arose from the sofa only briefly and went right back to bed when the games were over. According to the "Wellness Letter," it was this marathon of inactivity that nearly killed him, but, they cheerfully reported, he got to the hospital in time.

The newsletter went on in a reproving tone to point out that while this was an isolated case, "Long periods of inactivity don't do anybody much good as they tend to cause blood to settle in the body's nether regions."

Owing to his heroic proportions, Tom Watson Brown's nether regions are somewhere near Austell, but he was obviously concerned about the lethal implications of our mutually pleasurable pastime, watching television from a recumbent position.

In recent months, I have pursued this activity with such

vigor that my surly and desiccated spouse has taken to referring to me as "Mr. Couch Potato." (It is sad to think that, but for a teenage olfactory disorder that caused me to confuse the aroma of her lavishly applied Evening in Paris with pure passion, I could have avoided being trapped in this bleak and interminable union.)

By coincidence, I was something of a pioneer in discovering the dangers inherent in watching television while supine on the settee. In 1983, I read a paper on the subject to the prestigious South Cobb Chiropractic, Auto Upholstery and Video Rental Association, entitled "Television May Be Hazardous to Your Health." My research was grounded on personal experience in trying to watch the Playboy Channel on cable television although not a subscriber. The traumas reported resulted from Playboy's diabolical technique of sending a scrambled video signal to non-subscribers accompanied by a clear audio signal that permits the gasping and moaning to come through undiminished and undistorted. In a cunningly clever marketing maneuver, Playboy, knowing that thousands of middle-aged, sofa-bound males were twisting and turning while watching the scrambled signal, stabilizes the image for a split second or two and just as quickly resumes the scrambling. This, of course, causes hundreds of viewers, their prurient reveries abruptly ended, to fall off couches all over the United States and parts of Canada.

The paper was well received and resulted in wide acclaim and several offers for free five-dollar adjustments from various members of the Association.

In addition, many local clinicians this fall have reported countless patients who, after watching the Atlanta Falcons perform on television for successive Sundays, were exhibiting symptoms remarkably similar to narcolepsy. This is not unusual in that the Falcons themselves exhibited the same symptoms for the last half of the season.

The point in all of this is that with Super Sunday

approaching, Couch Potatoes of the world should be mindful of the fact that they are facing some real dangers.

As the National Safety Council advises, "Ninety percent of all accidents occur in the home." I think it was the National Safety Council. It may have been the Planned Parenthood League, but the point is to be careful on those couches.

*January 1987*

# THE AFGHAN BAG
# LADY AND
# OTHER FASHION
# ABERRATIONS

As sympathetic friends have long known, I have been locked for almost thirty years in a marriage to someone who enjoys an international reputation for bizarre fashion innovations. On the way to a recent Super Bowl party, I was more upset than those who bet the Giants wouldn't cover the spread when I suddenly realized that my leathery spouse was wearing an outfit consisting of boots, jodhpurs and a jacket that looked like the top half of a sleeping bag. My suggestion that she looked like an Afghan bag lady was dismissed with flared nostrils and a contemptuous snort. I tried to make light of it when we

reached the party by saying to the host, "We had to come in the VW, my wife's camel is still in the shop," but throughout the evening I could sense that almost all in attendance exuded sympathy for my obvious plight.

I say this by way of introduction to affirm that having lived this long with a kamikaze of *haute couture*, I am not easily shocked or surprised by any developing trends in female fashion. However, even my legendary tolerance for wretched excess has been severely tested by some of the mutant trends and fashion foibles now being affected by the softer set.

My recent stand against women dressing to the nines and then donning tennis shoes and socks was well received here and abroad, and my suggestion that textured hose gave their wearers the appearance of having suffered some exotic skin disease is widely credited with having caused the sale of those ugly aberrations to take a sharp downturn.

However, it seems that when one loathesome fad subsides, two more spring up to take its grisly place.

Nowadays, everywhere I go I see women wearing those ballet leg warmers. Not, as you might imagine, pulled up around their legs for the purpose of keeping them warm but worn, I suppose in some sort of perverse fashion statement, bunched up around the ankles, causing their owner to look like she just got off an elevator that had stopped too suddenly.

I have also spoken out against women who wear white hose and, at one point, wrote a strong letter to the editor urging legislation that would make them legal only for registered nurses and dental hygienists.

More recently, I have been appalled by women who, for reasons no one has been able to fathom, have begun wearing crew cuts. I suspect they are unwittingly placing their heads in the hands of hair dressers who secretly hate women. What other explanation can there be when a woman goes into a beauty parlor looking perfectly normal and comes out looking like Dobie Gillis.

In fairness, I should point out that not all of the outrageous trends infect the female population. One novelty that would test the gag reflex of a maggot is the recent epicene affectation among males to pierce their ears.

I was recently confounded by the sixteen-year-old son of a friend who turned up in my office with one pierced ear and a gold stud. "Don't you know," I warned, "that this business is just like marijuana."

He replied, "Huh?"

"Yes," I fulminated, "studies have shown that if you pierce one ear, you're likely to pierce the other. Before you know it, you have an overwhelming desire to apply a little lip gloss, and within a couple of months you find yourself skipping around the midtown area wearing pantyhose and a Laura Ashley blouse, singing 'I Enjoy Being a Girl.'"

He furrowed his brow mightily as if trying to pass some large thought and said, "Far out." Somehow his response seemed appropriate. Today's young people may be susceptible to silly trends, but you can't say they're not articulate.

*February 1987*

# I'D LIKE TO HELP YOU OUT. HOW DID YOU GET IN?

Well, I don't know about you, but I'm convinced that fashion rules the world. I know it has been a major influence in my life.

From the time I was but a pup I harbored a burning ambition (which, on occasion, throbbed as well) to pursue a career in the field of spot cleaning and blocking hats and even managed to obtain a full scholarship to the then famous L'Ecole de Chapeau in Cuthbert, Alabama, when lightning struck the world of fashion with the pronouncement that the bareheaded John F. Kennedy had rendered hats as dead as soccer.

Taken by surprise and bitterly disappointed, I grimly vowed that I would never again be left cold and goose-fleshed, sitting in the fashion tub after the water had drained. True to that resolve, from that day to this, I have remained in the words of even my severest foes "incredibly *au courant*," by devouring every issue of that bible of style and fashion to which my sinewy spouse so avidly subscribes, *W*.

This incredibly trendy arbiter of taste and good grooming is published bimonthly under an assumed name by its unlikely parent, *Women's Wear Daily*, a frumpy trade journal for those in the rag business. Over the years *W* has kept me on the cutting edge of the world of fashion, which is known to be subject to whimsy and caprice (not to be confused with the interior decorating firm by the same name).

Presented in living color in a full-sized newspaper format, *W* is perfect reading material for fashion-minded socialites who need to be on the crest of every fashion wave but find *Vogue, Harper's Bazaar* and the like—"with *all* that *writing*"— just too taxing mentally.

Eschewing text for the most part, *W* deals almost exclusively in photographs depicting what might be described by unsophisticated readers as "lifestyles of the rich and fatuous" captured as they caper about in their native habitats— society balls, restaurant or disco openings, coming outs of horsey-looking debutantes and a glittering and never-ending succession of similar self-congratulatory events.

Inside pages reveal the same old faces in new ensembles, like Nancy Kissinger, plowing through the high-society seas with the foot shorter and ever-dour Henry following in her wake looking like a dyspeptic troll who has been flushed from under a bridge wearing a tuxedo, and the ubiquitous Pat (Mrs. William F.) Buckley, who is featured so relentlessly that, one suspects, if she fails to appear in a single issue the publication will lose its bulk mailing permit.

My favorite *W* feature is the annual issue in which its editors reveal to a breathlessly expectant constituency of social lions from Sutton Place to East Marietta just what is "In" and "Out" for the year. Until I am able to clasp this definitive work to my anxious bosom, I, like all other *W* readers, am simply suspended in an opinionless fashion limbo.

In this year's fashion and style *pronunciamiento, W* decreed that bosoms are "in" though, from the accompanying photos, it seems clear that to be "in" they must be worn "out." Also "in" are Elizabeth Taylor (and her Grand Tetons), "being naughty at lunch" (which I take to mean staging food fights, drinking iced tea with the spoon still protruding from the glass and burping over one's demitasse), virginity (unless you're *really* being naughty at lunch), dancing the cha-cha and — get this — "wearing fake honorary decorations that turn over to reveal a photo of your dog."

*W* deemed the following to be "out": breast implants, which from the look of the high-fashion women in its pages, have been replaced by shoulder implants, aerobics, Sean Penn, Australia, Pat Robertson, "overgrown cities, like Atlanta," wine coolers and, to prove that *W* is not just fashion froth for simpleminded trend-spotters but really has a social conscience, "increasing executive salaries when a company is laying off employees." Workers of the world, unite, you have nothing to lose but your Guccis.

Finally, the editors have established a fashion and style purgatory so extreme it is designated as "The Out Palace," into whose nether regions they have summarily banished "Vanna White, Mario Cuomo, smoking between courses (which, apparently, is *de classe* even when trying to be 'naughty at lunch'), Prince Philip and hoop earrings." Frankly, I never really liked Prince Philip in those hoop earrings either.

So, Style-setters, the next time you're having one of those scruffy days when you feel like the world's a tuxedo and you're a pair of brown Hush Puppies, just snuggle up to a copy of *W.* You'll be glad you did.

*March 1987*

# BAD DAY
# IN BEULAH LAND

Jim, Tammy Faye, what in heaven's name is going on?
For those members of the reading public who may have
been in a spiritual coma for the last few years and are blanking
out at the mention of the names of televangelism's biggest and
brightest stars—Jim and Tammy Faye Bakker of the *PTL Club*—
they should know that Jim Bakker, that fund-raising, God-
praising guru of the vast PTL television ministry, abruptly
resigned last week after confessing to have yielded to an
isolated temptation of the flesh in Florida seven years back and
then succumbing to blackmail to keep the episode under

cover, so to speak.

As a longtime, faithful and avid observer and commentator with respect to the Bakkers (the second k, some suggest, stands for *kash*), I have been receiving calls from sea to shining sea wailing about this latest drama in the never-ending spiritual saga of Jim and Tammy Faye.

By way of information to those cable TV addicts with Type-A remote control devices, who never light on a channel long enough to learn the names of all the talking heads bobbing about, Jim Bakker is the dapper little preacher who looks like an ordained chipmunk and his wife, Tammy Faye, is the stocky blonde who looks like an honor graduate of Our Lady of Perpetual Mascara.

Their show, a quintessential example of successful electronic plate-passing, raised more than $125 million last year for worthy enterprises like sales of dolls, building of hotels, a miniature railroad and Christendom's largest and most infamous water slide—all combined in sort of a grandiose spiritual retreat in Fort Mill, South Carolina, in the manner of Six Flags Over Heaven.

Although the fortunes of the Bakkers and the *PTL Club* clearly thrive in the choppy seas of chaos and crisis, I was downcast when it was revealed a couple of weeks ago that Tammy Faye would be off the air for a while to be treated for drug dependency. I has long been concerned about a Maybelline overdose and really was not surprised that the lachrymose songbird, who perpetually hovers on the brink of bursting into either song or tears, may have needed some prescription medicine to keep up with the frantic pace involved in any enterprise that stays on the air as much as the *PTL Club* and is required to keep bringing in the sheaves in such staggering numbers to buy all that air time. The pressures would not be unlike those encountered by rock-and-roll stars in the equally intense and high-financed secular sector. In fact, it seemed to me that the success of this spiritual soap opera must thrive upon, if not require, crisis after crisis to stir the souls (and empty the pockets) of the vast TV following who respond with periodic cash avalanches.

But things got really bad in Beulah Land when Jim confessed to his clerical error and simply threw in the tel-evangelical towel. If what he reported is all he has done, I think he may be being a little hard on himself.

Now he says the real reason he left PTL like a mailbag leaving a rail siding is because of a threatened "hostile take-over" attempt by a fellow televangelist from his own denomina-tion, identified by his lawyer as the Right Reverend Jimmy Swaggart.

Over the years the Bakkers have been battered and bedeviled by marital problems, ebbs in the cash flow, harass-ment and pressure by various groups and relentless yapping at their heels by the *Charlotte Observer*, which is always keen to know what they are *doing* with all that manna. However, each low point seemed to be a springboard for new highs and increased donations from their devoted electronic parishioners.

Whether you agree with their style, dogma or approach, it seems clear, at least as clear as $125 million in contributions a year, that the Bakkers were furnishing something that their following needed and, more important, very badly wanted, and they deserve, at a minimum, some current compassion, under-standing and forgiveness from that following. They have weathered a lot of storms in the past, and there is no reason to believe that this, their biggest crisis, won't lead to even more towering triumphs. (Think in terms of a giant ferris wheel to glory.)

Unless there are more grisly shoes yet to drop in terms of disclosure by Brother Jim, I'm convinced that the Bakkers will be back, storming the beaches like MacArthur, wading through the spiritual breakwaters in triumphant return to abide (and shear) their forgiving flocks.

In the meantime, they might well abide by Chapter 26, Verse 20 of Isaiah, "Hide thyself as it were for a little moment, until the indignation be overpast."

*March 1987*

# SLIPPING BENEATH THE SURFACE ON THE GOOD SHIP MONKEY BUSINESS

If Gary Hart can talk his way out of this bedroom farce, he deserves to be President. Moreover, I think he will be a shoo-in for the 1987 Alex Hawkins "That's My Story and I'm Sticking to It" Award.

The entire caper could be a screenplay for a Three Stooges movie. Hart's friend, William Broadhurst, says he, Donna Rice and another woman, the missing and mysterious Ms. Armandt, entered Hart's house by a rear entrance to view Hart's new deck. (I don't know how the deck looked, but from the photo of Donna Rice in swimming trunks that came over the

AP wire, *she* certainly doesn't have any structural flaws.) Broadhurst says he and Armandt left by the rear door. Hart and Rice, he said, left by the front door to join them. The *Miami Herald* said Hart and Rice left in Hart's car and returned about two hours later and went in the front door. Broadhurst says that all four later returned to Hart's house — Broadhurst and Armandt entering through the rear door, Hart and Rice through the front door. Then, Broadhurst says, ten minutes later, he, Rice and Armandt all left by the rear door to go back to his house, leaving Hart alone.

Front door, back door, side door, trap door, it all gets a bit confusing, and the confusion is further compounded by a boat trip to Bimini on the good ship *Monkey Business*.

Through all of this, I see a *Miami Herald* reporter who looks a little like Curly in the Three Stooges, looking over the transom and going "Nyuk, Nyuk, Nyuk" while Larry and Moe are bumping into and pummeling each other covering the back door.

Senator Hart ( formerly "Hartpence" which is, I believe, German for "hot pants") hasn't had much success in clearing all of this up for the media. Taking into account the seventy-two-hour silence by his wife, I think he's having an even more difficult time explaining it to her. It rivals the challenge once described by former New York Yankee pitcher Jim Bouton, who, when asked what was the most difficult thing he had ever had to do as a professional baseball player, replied, "Trying to explain to my wife why *she* needed a shot of penicillin for *my* kidney infection."

Almost as bad as the political kamikaze flight Hart is now making is the public humiliation offered by the toothsome Ms. Rice with her gratuitous comment regarding her feelings for the fifty-year-old Hart — "I don't know if he was attracted to me, but there was nothing between us. I am more attracted to younger men." Oh, sharper than a serpent's tooth.

## THE SASS MENAGERIE

If he and the parties to the transaction seem to be confused to the point of doing variations on Abbott and Costello's "Who's on First?" routine, there are also reports that the befuddlement is bipartisan. A leak from the White House revealed that President Reagan, while watching Senator Gephardt on television, turned abruptly to Mrs. Reagan, and said, "Mommy, who is this Gephardt? You don't suppose that fellow Hartpence has changed his name again?"

*May 1987*

# THE PERILS OF CUSTOM-TAILORED GENES

If current developments continue unchecked, biology may soon be taught as an engineering course.

Accompanying a recent news account, there appeared a photo of what looked to be an astronaut dusting a small patch of strawberries with "genetically altered bacteria." While saliva glands on fruit lovers everywhere went into a state of gridlock, the scientists involved giddily proclaimed that the altered bacteria would prevent frost on crops. I would like to think that if whipped cream is not available, most fruit-loving Americans, given a choice between frost and bacteria on their strawberries, would go with frost by at least ten to one.

The experiment took place in — where else — California and was hailed as a major step toward an era in which "advanced tools of molecular biology" would be applied even more widely in agriculture. To hear the scientists involved gloat over the crop-dusting, you would have thought it the biggest breakthrough since George Washington Carver accidentally discovered peanut butter. Haven't these eggheads ever seen *The Little Shop of Horrors*? This stuff could get out of hand — "Little Lamar, eat your vegetables . . . before they eat you."

My mind's eye flashes toward a tableau at Chez Quiche where some waiter hovering over a table simpers, "Will you take your bacteria over the compote or on the side?"

I was on record against bacteria even before they started genetically altering it. As early as 1980, I publicly urged mandatory testing to root out public officials and athletes suspected of using buttermilk or yogurt.

This tinkering with nature has simply gone too far. Every morning edition brings some new breakthrough in steroid-stuffed chicken, beef or offensive tackles, DNA alterations, and high-tech conception. The prestigious *Cobb County Journal of Genetics and Drag Racing* recently revealed that in 1986 more babies were conceived in laboratories than at drive-in movies. If these science-fiction modes of procreation continue apace, half the population will wind up sending Father's Day cards to some petri dish in Southern California.

Man's preoccupation with improving on nature by scientific means goes back at least as far as Mary Shelley's account of Dr. Frankenstein jump-starting the monster with lightning, and I predict that current attempts with designer genes will have the same unhappy result.

It's not wise to fool Mother Nature. All this talk about altering the DNA so as to root out diseases, rickets, fallen arches and facial hair represents a dangerous assault on the natural order. People weren't meant to order babies like they buy stereo components—"We'd like the male model 211, with blue eyes, dimples and hold the cowlick."

What kind of world would it be if everyone looked like Robert Redford?

On the other hand, no one would look like Yasir Arafat. Maybe we shouldn't be so quick to criticize.

*May 1987*

# TIME IS
# FUNNY

As I plowed through some sixteen pounds of Sunday news-paper, tacking carefully through the sea of cheery AIDS stories, the never-ending and numbing news from Nicaragua, and the flotsam and jetsam of gratuitous catalogs that bob about in the waters that must be navigated in search of the wonderfully lurid and pulse-quickening lingerie ads that would likely bring color to Hugh Hefner's sallow and sunken cheeks, I came upon what at first blush seemed to be a bargain of the first order for those seeking a status wristwatch. The advertisement bleated "Rolex" and "$133," causing my bargain-hunting juices to stir in greedy anticipation.

Though I myself have an aging but serviceable $125 Accutron ("Railroad Approved") timepiece, I was tempted by the offer as I am not unaware that there exists considerable status in owning certain watches and that high in the pantheon of these showpieces is the mighty Rolex.

In the wake (hold on queasy reader and we'll soon sail through these tiresome nautical metaphors, which—the nurse thinks—were brought on by a mild overdose of Cutty Sark) of the spiritual soap opera offered by Jim and Tammy Faye Bakker and their pastoral peccadillos, the legendary panache of the Rolex was even acknowledged in song as Ray Stevens posed the musical question "Would Jesus Wear a Rolex on His Television Show?" The rhetorical barb, as all of us who follow the plethora of televangelists now infesting the air waves know, was directed at the Right Reverend James ("Jimmy") Swaggart, whose shiny Rolex approximates the size of a weather station in Greenland and is thought by some to be a bit gaudy for a man of the cloth (though Jimmy, in his own defense, points out tersely that some cloth can be right gaudy, too, indicating tattersall and madras to, in his words, "name just a few").

I don't want to get drawn into any ideological arguments on the question of appropriate timepieces for our spiritual leaders (though I would observe in passing that it would be difficult for the Pope to wear a pocket watch). I just brought the subject up in the first place (for those of you who haven't abandoned this exposition altogether in search of the lingerie ads) to say that I was mildly tempted to spring for $133 worth of status. A closer reading of the ad copy, however, revealed to my incredulous eye (the right one is incredulous, the left believes almost everything it sees, including, for example, World Federation Wrestling and claims by cable TV hucksters that "Fortunes can be made by buying foreclosed real estate with no money down") that this overstuffed stainless steel-and-gold status symbol was going down not for $133 but for

$133 *per month* for twenty-four months which, unless my multiplication is off, comes to a tidy $3,192 (plus appplicable sales tax).

Now, I'm as much for status as the next man (maybe even more as I note that the next man is wearing one of those digital watches found at truck-stop counters that pulses "Go Dawgs" every second), but three grand for a watch that is fat, heavy and ugly to boot is going a bit too far for me.

Consequently, I'm advising those status seekers who come clamoring to my chambers for counsel to buy a Timex and use their savings to (i) invest in a pair of Gucci loafers and wear them without socks (nothing says status like hairy ankles and little gold dingles on your shoes); (ii) rent a car phone, which you can do for less than $133 a month, and impress the stew out of other motorists who think you're doing big deals when you're really just trying to be Caller Number Ten on some radio station and win free tickets to a water slide in Smyrna; or (iii) have your VW Beetle fitted out with one of those Rolls Royce fronts and get a little sign for the window that says "Dork on Board" (maybe with the Rolls Royce front you won't even need the sign).

Besides, you really don't deserve too much status if you have to buy your watch "on time." (There may be a pun in there somewhere, but we'll just have to wait for it to surface.)

*June 1987*

# STANDING IN THE NEED OF PRAYER

I have never fully appreciated the ultimate possibilities of the cliché "A marriage made in heaven" until I learned that Melvin Belli was joining forces with Jim and Tammy Faye Bakker. Who says there is no God? Who says God has no sense of humor? Who says there's no good comedy on television anymore?

I think I can say without fear of contradiction (unless, of course, my wife is within earshot) that Melvin Belli is to the law what Jim and Tammy Faye are to religion.

The problem with this lively holy war to date has been

that the players haven't been evenly matched. What chance does the munchkin-like Jim Bakker have against the imposing girth of Jerry Falwell, whose sincere baritone always sounds to me as though he is dictating to a stonecutter. He has that big, booming sonority that some folks call an "FM voice" while Brother Bakker's scratchy little midwestern intonation sounds tinny and whimperish by comparison, even when supplemented by the steady sobbing of Our Lady of Perpetual Mascara, the ever-lachrymose Tammy Faye.

But now, the True Church has invited that spiritual Titan, Melvin Belli, to join their Angel Band, and the odds, it seems to me, are becoming a little more even. All this spiritual circus really needed was some first-rate legal histrionics, and Belli is just the man to provide that. According to Belli, Jerry Falwell is in serious danger of being smote hip and thigh, and while I don't know exactly what that involves, it sounds unpleasant and painful.

To keep this fracas out of court but still in the public eye, I'd like to suggest that World Federation Wrestling consider the possibility of outfitting Jerry and Melvin in leather athletic supporters and staging a sumo wrestling match with the winner getting clear title to the PTL's Six Flags Over Heaven in Fort Mill, South Carolina. If the fray should end in a draw, they might let Falwell bring Sally Struthers and pit her against Tammy Faye in a "cry-off" to decide the match.

Frankly, I have long noted the ringing similarities in both style and substance between TV preachers and trial lawyers. As a corporate lawyer friend once observed, "It's refreshing to see how much faith trial lawyers have in themselves, particularly in these troubled times when so many people believe in no God at all."

Trial lawyers and publicity are like moths and flames. They can't stand on the sidelines long if there is an opportunity for the spotlight and are marvelously undaunted by the possibility of public pratfalls. Belli rushing into this debacle with a rapacious gleam in his rheumy eye reminds me of the old story in which a trial attorney, following the jury argument by his opposition, jumped up in front of the jury, hitched his pants, set his jaw and said, "My opponent has been before you for forty-five minutes making a complete ass of himself. Well, now it's *my* turn."

With all these good publicity possibilities a number of questions occur to me: (1) How long will it be before Barbara Walters schedules an interview with Tammy Faye?; (2) When will Congress realize they're boring the populace stiff with the Nicaragua nonsense and turn to more fertile grounds, staging televised hearings on the *PTL Club* imbroglio?

And, speaking of Barbara Walters, she did her usual deft and delicate job with the Donna Rice interview, but when she asked ever so sweetly, "Donna, were you sweeping with Gary Hart?" I thought it would have been wonderful if the comely Ms. Rice had responded, "Well, we swept the patio and were going to do the front stoop, but that's when all the reporters swooped in."

Onward, Christian soldiers.

*June 1987*

# CROESUS, MY HOW YOU'VE CHANGED

Perhaps one of the most anxious moments in modern times is the lapse between asking an old friend whom you have not seen for some time the question "How's your wife?" and getting the answer. I ask the question almost by reflex and then mentally bite my knuckle and worry that he's going to pull a face, look down at his shoes and say: (1) "We've been divorced for three years"; (2) "She went back to law school and filed her own divorce"; or (3) "I'm living with my dental hygienist." (The wonderful thing about Henny Youngman was that when you asked him that question he always said, "Compared to what?")

I bring this up because someone mentioned to me the other day that he was reluctant to ask after my sinewy spouse because I hadn't written anything about her in many months. I was happy to report to him that the union has not yet been put asunder. It continues to be, as Jimmy Durante used to say in describing his bandleader's job, "hanging by a tread."

My friend looked a little dubious and suggested that if she didn't surface soon in my literary endeavors, he might send the authorities around to dig up my patio.

Actually, we should be separated. I should be living in our home, and she should be in the Intensive Care Wing of the State Home for the Verbally Dyslexic in Valdosta. However, I wouldn't dream of splitting up. Aside from the fact that during a distant fit of passion I put the house in her name, I'm also hooked for the long haul because I simply can't wait to hear what bizarre utterance she will come up with next.

I have long been convinced that English is, for my wiry mate of twenty-nine years, a second language. We have yet to discover her first.

I have already publicly affirmed that her curiously colorful but unconventional speech patterns result not from lack of brain power—she is as smart as any 101-pound person I know—but rather a monumentally bad ear.

Her mangling of our mother tongue takes many forms. Sometimes all of the words are right, but the sentiment sought to be expressed is as fuzzy as a cheap sweater. Speaking of a friend of ours, she proclaimed, "Cynthia is so much like herself she doesn't even know it." If one is not listening carefully, such an observation will appear to make sense. However, if it actually registers in the conscious level and is analyzed, it will cause blurred vision and a ringing sensation in one's ears.

She recently told our friend Allison that, "Nothing goes past me with you." He struggled for a moment trying to glean the essence of that offering, but ultimately his eyes glazed over like a sugar doughnut and his lips began to move wordlessly.

Some of her sayings, though complete sentences, are so cryptic as to defy comprehension— "I can only do what I try"; "My blood is too fat for this"; "You could not discern his demeanor"; "He just eludes essence."

Others are just about fifteen degrees off: "He would leave no leaf unturned"; "That fellow is very unsophisticated; he seems almost like a clout"; "I don't squelch on my bets"; "Byron likes to sit around and pontiferate"; "It's a mute question."

No cliché is safe from her maladroit touch. In the space of three days she said something was "hot as Croesus," later described a house as having been "dark as Croesus" and told someone a day later that a town was "as far as Croesus." Croesus never imagined that his riches could be counted in similes.

Sometimes her utterings sound as though they carry with them an undercurrent of folk wisdom but, on analysis, simply slither into the surreal.

We went to a commercial art gallery recently, and the director came up and mildly remonstrated with us for not having been by for some time. My wife established good eye contact with the poor woman and said, "He moves the best who yanks the hardest." The gallery owner slumped visibly, her brow furrowed and one eye seemed to drift toward her nose. I'm sure she thought she had suffered a small stroke.

Frankly, I don't think even the folks in Valdosta would be equal to the challenge. But, on the other hand, as our daughter once speculated after her mother had uttered a particularly mind-bruising malapropism, "Wouldn't it be funny if when she got old and senile everything started coming out right?"

Indeed. As funny as Croesus.

*June 1987*

# THOSE PEDALING
# PANSIES

As that great American philosopher, I think it was Ralph Waldo Emerson (it was either Ralph Waldo Emerson or Troy Donahue; I always get those two mixed-up) once said, "There are fads and there are fads." In one pithy statement, he summed up, I think, a notion of cosmic proportions. The main pith in his thoughtful observation is that fads can range from mere silliness to the life-threatening. We have all seen some aberrant behavior pass from fad to craze to menace.

A mere fad can be a bit of asininity no more grave than some middle-aged man wearing a gold neck chain hanging about his fat, greasy wattles, women wearing tennis shoes and socks to work, or people putting silly yellow signs in their automobile windows to draw attention to the fact that (1) their mother-in-law is in the trunk, (2) they brake for possums, or (3) someone dopey is "on board."

In the "craze" category, i.e., stupid but only mildly threatening to one's person or society, we have things like men wearing earrings, Mexican beer, those blimp-type tires that the mechanically deranged put on jacked-up vehicles and the like.

In the category of "menace," there repose such unsavory and life-threatening fads as skydiving, pit bulls, and cycling in packs on the public streets and highways.

It is this last bit of deviant and dangerous behavior that I now propose to cover in this preliminary working paper for a more extended work scheduled to appear in the prestigious *Harvard Journal of Tacky Behavior and Apartment Hunters' Guide* some time this fall.

My exposé is prompted by the fact that every time I venture out on a weekend I find the public streets clogged with gangs of pesky bike riders racing about in fruity costumes on skinny, sinister-looking space-age cycles.

Many of us old enough to recall World War II will remember quaint machines called "bicycles" (though I don't mean to suggest in any meaningful way a connection between bicycles and World War II), which were entertaining bits of machinery with models for both sexes. The boy's version was made with a horizontal bar from the seat to the handle bars while the girl's came without a bar though, frankly, the logic of this design was never readily apparent to me. The machines featured baskets on the front for carrying things about, brakes on the pedals for retarding forward motion and seats that were designed to accommodate normal human bottoms for sustained stretches of time. Cyclists who wished to indicate they were serious about the sport did so by removing the basket and both fenders and attaching a playing card with a clothespin to the rear wheel

strut so that the spokes would sound like a motor.

The new machines have nothing in common with their predecessors. They are unisex (like everything else these days) and sport humped-over handlebars with little levers for brakes, pencil-thin tires and a seat the size of your average three-iron.

One has to believe that anyone attracted to such a curious-looking piece of equipment must have some serious personality quirks of their own. This is certainly reinforced by the goofy outfits currently being affected by the modern American biker. First, they are wearing special shoes, biking gloves (the only outdoor sport that hasn't come up with special gloves is sunbathing), little plastic hats that look like reinforced Tupperware and, worst of all, sissy-looking spandex Bermuda shorts that can be gotten into only with shoehorns or by jumping into them from a high place. These elastic britches are not only skintight; they are also padded in the aft section (see "seat the size of your average three-iron" above) and, according to medical authorities, provoke a form of diaper rash so incredibly unsightly and grisly that young hospital interns and residents blanch and grow faint at the sight of it. I would suggest that anyone who enjoys pedaling great distances on a seat that a squirrel couldn't comfortably perch on is in real danger of abandoning his regular job and going into choreography full time.

As currently practiced, it is clearly not a solitary sport, and the bikers, perhaps because of the sissy shorts, seem to run about in packs, seeing how close they can come to walkers and joggers and how much traffic they can obstruct. Worse yet, if any motorist presumes to honk at them, they fly into a towering rage, flaring their nostrils and looking as menacing as someone can look in those silly-looking outfits.

I don't know why they have such a low boiling point. My guess is it's those bicycle seats.

*July 1987*

# THAT SUSHI IS
# HARD TO SWALLOW

On a recent trip to Los Angeles a lawyer friend of mine there offered to take me to dinner at a sushi bar, and I eagerly accepted. I assumed we were going to one of those Japanese restaurants that is a combination between a catfish house and the old Ed Sullivan Show, where wiry waiters juggle kitchen utensils, shrimp and condiments and stage periodic grease fires on a communal griddle.

I enjoy those outings in that the theatre is entertaining, and the food, if not cooked sufficiently for one's liking, can be slipped surreptitiously back on the griddle at the end of a

chopstick and rendered edible in time. I have always belonged to the school of gastronomic thought that if something couldn't be battered, fried and chewed, it was not a legitimate foodstuff. In the outlawed category would fall such titans of queasiness as raw oysters, boiled okra and that darling of bridge clubs and family reunions alike, aspic.

Like a lamb entering an abattoir, I was led by my friend into a small Japanese eatery as antiseptic in appearance as the inside of a Frigidaire. Everything was black, white and lacquered, and the menu, which featured esoteric entrees such as "Maguro, Toro, Hammachi and Saba," offered no clue as to the quivering and slithery selections that were soon to be placed right under our noses.

Noting my rising state of befuddlement, my companion airily offered to order for both of us and muttered a series of Oriental incantations to the eager and beaming waiter.

I should have been suspicious at the outset, as California is widely known as an incubator for every form of weird comestible ranging from tofu, frozen yogurt and bean sprouts to trail mix and granola. In fact, some savants have suggested that granola is itself an appropriate metaphor for California in that "Everything that ain't fruits or flakes is nuts." However, I was simply not prepared for the platter of colorful, slippery delicacies that was placed before me. It turns out that sushi consists exclusively of uncooked fish and fish by-products arranged in colorful little balls or geometric patterns. Of course it's colorful — the stuff hasn't been near a stove. Suppressing an involuntary shiver, I said to my companion, "I hate to be a chicken of the sea, but I'm not eating any of that stuff. If God wanted us to eat raw fish, He would have given us nine lives."

"Oh," she said, "you really ought to try the tobiko; it's flying-fish roe, and the bright orange eggs are firm and salty and almost explode with flavor when you bite them."

"Not in this lifetime, Jacques Cousteau breath," I gagged. "Maybe if Mr. Moto over there could zap these beauties in the microwave I'd be willing to give them a nibble around the edges."

Rolling her eyes to convey her dismay at being with such a culinary yahoo, my friend dived into the briny offerings with the gusto of a bear catching salmon in the Columbia River while I sought to stave off hunger pangs with a pack of stale Rolaids.

It is a staggering notion to think that there are grown people out there paying $19.95 for a mess of codfish colons artfully arranged to look like a platter of sweetheart roses. I have formed a committee of concerned citizens to press for legislation requiring warning labels on sushi bar menus reading something like, "The Surgeon General has determined that gobbling uncooked marine offal will cause permanent damage to your gag reflex and may turn your liver into a doorstop."

While California is obviously the hotbed of this kamikaze cuisine (there is even a combination French and sushi restaurant on Rodeo Drive called Chez Hepatitis), evidence exists that the trend is spreading. I have overheard yuppies in downtown elevators rapturously extolling the virtues of squid spleens and carp chitterling to one another and even heard that the fishy fad had reached Cobb County. However, I checked out the Cobb County rumor, and it turned out to be a false alarm. It seems that the deep-fat fryer at the Rio Vista in Marietta was on the blink, and some of the catfish came out undercooked.

However, to demonstrate just how widespread the threat has become, I learned from a friend in Birmingham that sushi has even spread to darkest Alabama. "The only difference," he said, "is that in Alabama we call it 'bait.'"

*September 1987*

# SEEMS TO ME I'VE HEARD THAT SONG BEFORE

In a wonderfully ironic sidebar to the confirmation hearings by the Senate Judiciary Committee on Judge Robert Bork, the Chairman of the Committee, Senator Joe Biden, is having to scurry around and defend his own flanks from those charging him with rampant plagiarizing from the speeches of others during his Presidential campaign.

Biden was first charged with purloining some lyrical phrases (including gestures) from a taped television commercial of British Labor Party candidate Neil Kinnock (who went down in flames to Margaret Thatcher despite his lyricism).

Mr. Kinnock had asked in his commercial why his Welsh ancestors had failed to succeed, saying, "Did they lack talent? Those people who could sing and play and recite and write poetry? Those people who could make wonderful, beautiful things with their hands? Those people who could dream dreams, see visions? Why didn't they get it? Was it because they were weak? Those people who could work eight hours underground and then come up and play football?"

Senator Biden, in a not-so-instant replay during an Iowa debate, referring to his Irish relatives and answering the same rhetorical question, waxed larcenous with, "Those same people who read poetry and wrote poetry and taught me how to sing verse? Is it because they didn't work hard? My ancestors, who worked in the coal mines of northern Pennsylvania and would come up after twelve hours and play football for four hours?"

Though Biden's ancestors (his father was a Chevrolet dealer) did appear to work harder than Kinnock's and play more football, many were struck by the similarity of their prose.

Other Kinnock phrases found their way into the same Biden debate. Kinnock, further explaining why his tribe did not succeed, said "It was because there was no platform upon which they could stand." Biden, defending his footless forebears, said, "It's because they didn't have a platform upon which to stand."

According to newspaper accounts, Senator Biden began his Iowa remarks by saying that the ideas had come to him spontaneously on his way to the debate.

His flowery campaign rhetoric began to grow a little more red-faced when he was charged several days later with lifting phrases and even larger chunks from speeches by John and Robert Kennedy.

In 1968, Senator Kennedy said, "The gross national product does not allow for the health of our children, the quality of their education or the joy of their play. It does not include the beauty of our poetry or the strength of our marriages, the intelligence of our public debate or the integrity of our public officials. It measures neither our wit nor our courage, neither our wisdom nor our devotion to our country. It measures everything, in short, except that which makes life worthwhile, and it can tell us everything about America except why we are proud that we are Americans."

Biden, in a California convention speech, after saying in the opening that he wanted to tell the audience "what is on my mind," soared with, "It cannot measure the health of our children, the quality of their education, the joy of their play. . . . It doesn't measure the beauty of our poetry, the strength of our marriages, the intelligence of our public debate, the integrity of our public officials. It counts neither our wit nor our wisdom, neither our compassion nor our devotion to our country. That bottom line can tell us everything about our lives except that which makes life worthwhile, and it can tell us everything about America except that which makes us proud to be Americans."

Joe Biden may well be to public speaking what Jesse James was to banking. Who knows where the silver-tongued Senator will strike next? The following interview might not be too fanciful:

**Interviewer:**   Senator, what do you say to those critics who have charged you with appropriating the words of others in your speeches without attribution?

**Biden:**   Some have at first for poets passed, turn critics next, and prove plain fools at last. Some can neither for poets nor critics pass as heavy mule is neither horse nor ass.

# THE SASS MENAGERIE

| | |
|---|---|
| **Interviewer:** | Didn't Alexander Pope write that? |
| **Biden:** | No, I don't think so. It came to me this morning while I was teasing my hair. |
| **Interviewer:** | Will this distract you from your fight against Judge Bork's confirmation to the Supreme Court? |
| **Biden:** | We shall fight on the beaches, we shall fight on the landing grounds, we shall fight in the fields and in the streets, we shall fight in the hills; we shall never surrender. |
| **Interviewer:** | Haven't I heard that somewhere before? |
| **Biden:** | Perhaps. I used it in a speech earlier this year. |
| **Interviewer:** | Then you are chairing the hearings in an evenhanded manner? |
| **Biden:** | With malice toward none; with charity for all; with firmness in the right, as God gives us to see the right. |
| **Interviewer:** | I *know* I've heard that before. |
| **Biden:** | You couldn't have; I just thought it up. |

I suspect the ship of state will sail on even if Biden's antics keep Bork from being confirmed. Frankly, I am concerned about the possible loss of prestige to the court that might result from adding a member whose last name sounds like the noise made by a dog with a sinus condition. However, it is a tad ironic that Bork is being so rigorously grilled on matters of principle by a man who may have stolen more lines than Milton Berle.

Biden, admiring a friend's quip, might well say, "I wish I had said that." And the friend, plagiarizing an old joke, could reply, "Don't worry, you will."

*September 1987*

**131**

# UP AND DOWN WITH THE INS AND OUTS

In the movie *The Jerk* (I've always been a devotee of art films), Steve Martin, playing the title role, runs out into the street screaming, "The telephone books are here! The telephone books are here!" after finding his name among the listings.

Such is the reaction in my household during the early days of January each year after we have waited with bated breath (except for those of us who keep packets of Sen-Sen handy) for the arrival of the annual issue of society's *arbiter elegantiarum, W,* revealing what is "In" and what is "Out" for the coming year.

# THE SASS MENAGERIE

Whenever possible, I try to get to the mail first in that my sinewy spouse has a vicious habit of sifting through the postal offerings and putting our copy of *Victoria's Secrets* in the trash masher if she gets to the mailbox before I do. (She tells friends it's for my own good, claiming that when I'm looking at those young hard-bodies pouting around in their teddies, she can hear me wheezing clear across the house.)

So it was with trembling hand one recent morning that I retrieved the eagerly awaited *W* issue from the twenty pounds of catalog flotsam and jetsam accompanying it and rushed back into the house bellowing, "*W* is here! *W* is here!"

My furrowed bride, as anxious as I for any sign or word from Gotham City as to what is socially up to snuff, drew nigh unto me, and, over steaming mugs of her justifiably famous instant coffee, we eagerly devoured *W*'s thoughtful pronunciamentos.

Under the "In" column an early entry was "Having eighteen-year-old legs no matter how old you are." My wife wondered aloud if she had missed news of some transplant breakthrough while I stayed mum and pondered the eternal wisdom of the maxim that "It's best never to tell your wife her hose are baggy unless you are absolutely sure she's wearing hose."

On the "Outs" are: Jackie O ("for being rude at charity functions"), Andree Putman ("the French decorator"), Prince Edward ("because he does nothing but organize silly TV shows"), and "the pushy self-promoters": Malcolm Forbes, Liz Taylor, Gary Hart, all real-estate developers, Pee-Wee Herman and, in a stinging setback for *détente*, Raisa and Mikhail Gorbachev. To show that its lists were not slighting the sectarian social set, *W* also pronounced as "out" Tammy Faye and Jim Bakker and, demonstrating a wonderfully even-handed ecumenism, Cardinal O'Connor, thus making it near impossible for the three of them to get a good table at La Grenouille during 1988.

**133**

"In" are thank-you notes (another small victory for the Junior League), women wearing men's fragrances (there's something about an Aqua Velva girl), food fights at corporate lunches (small wonder the stock market is in a state of free fall), and English country houses, which will come as a keen disappointment to the social set in fashionable East Marietta, where second homes have been tending more toward RVs and trailers.

In a revelation certain to cause consternation in the ranks of pubescent society felines, kittens are pronounced "in" but cats are declared "out." Bringing your dog to dinner in a French restaurant is "in," but I would caution pet lovers not to try it in Chinese eateries, lest the next day's menu feature "Sweet and Sour Spot."

In a refreshing return to traditional values, W declares among the "in" french fries, apple pie, freckles and — get this — Lake Rabun, Georgia. Next thing you know, we'll be seeing Avedon photos in Vogue and Harper's Bazaar of In-siders Nadine de Rothschild and Pat Buckley chatting over a No. 2 can of Vienna sausage down at the Chez Clayton Bait, Tackle and Video Rental.

Call-waiting, I'm delighted to report, is "out." I'm sick to death of hearing those little rat barks when I'm talking to someone on the phone. Boxer shorts are pronounced "forever in," bringing back for me vivid recollections of my father's sage advice as he put his college-bound son on a southbound Greyhound in 1954, saying, "Boy, always try to get a seat by the window, and don't let that bunch down at Mercer make you room with anybody who wears them jockey shorts."

The old man never read W, but he knew the "ins" and "outs."

*January 1988*

# SOME OF MY BEST
# FRIENDS ARE WOMEN

As I sat one recent evening at a Carter Presidential Library gathering during a convocation of former First Ladies commemorating the role of women in the celebration of the United States Constitution, I wondered aloud, "If Alan Alda and Phil Donahue are so super-sensitive to feminist issues, why aren't they here?"

"Don't mind him," my wife said to the lady sitting next to me. "He goes on like this all the time." Indeed, the saccharin and sychophantic Donahue and Alda were nowhere to be found while I, often unjustly pilloried as a male chauvinist, was asked to serve on the prestigious planning committee for this dinner along with — get this — only two other males. One was Andy Fisher of WSB, and the other was Jack H. Watson, Jr., an obscure operative in the Carter Administration, whose rudimentary sensitivity to the feminist movement was learned at my knee while he practiced law in our chambers. "He was probably just invited for his looks," I muttered.

"Really," my wife said, leaning across me to speak to the lady again, "he'll calm down when the program begins."

The program was a great treat for everyone. The superwomen of Atlanta and from all points of the compass had gathered to enjoy a panel of former First Ladies discussing throbbing women's issues of the day. Most of the high-powered ladies had submissive husbands in tow. I, of course, was there as a member of the prestigious planning committee.

The panel consisted of Sarah Weddington, a charming Texas law professor, as moderator, Rosalyn Carter, Lady Bird Johnson, and, filling in for an ailing Betty Ford, Liz Carpenter, journalist and former Press Secretary in the Johnson White House.

All of the panelists were in good form, exhibiting great presence and strong insights. However, it is fair to say that Liz Carpenter absolutely stole the show. (For some reason I relate in the strongest way to people who are grey-haired and soft and cuddly.) She opened modestly by saying that she was a poor substitute for Betty Ford. Even setting aside fierce party differences (Carpenter is an avowed Yellow-Dog Democrat), she said she was otherwise no match for the former First Lady, noting that "having me representing Betty Ford is a lot like asking Tammy Faye Bakker to sit in for Sister Teresa."

While the other panelists were extolling the virtues of highway beautification, housing for the poor, women as changing role models, Liz Carpenter was taking the button off her political foil and going after the Republicans. She said she didn't like Bob Dole's personality much, observing, "He has a pit bull for a lap dog." She went on to inform us that Bush was so embarrassed by his Iowa showing that he flew back on Air Force Three.

Finally joining the rest of the ladies on the general subject with which the panel was grappling, the lively Ms. Liz quoted one of my heroes, Senator Alben Barkley who, according to her, once said, "There's no profession in the world that women haven't improved, especially the oldest." Alben, I thought, while on the right track, could have been a bit more sensitive.

Except for the marvelously salty Liz (whose recently released biography, *Getting Better All the Time*, I plan to rush out and buy), the panelists were gracious, restrained and fairly low key. They did begin a good deal of tub-thumping for the ERA toward the end of the discussion, urging all of us to go out and flog our legislators through that gauntlet again.

As the crowd was leaving the meeting room for the dinner that followed the panel discussion, a subdued husband behind me, apparently a boxing fan, said quietly, "The women are way ahead on points." Indeed, as a doctor friend and I waited outside the rest rooms for our feminists to return, another friend, Ann Klamon (not her real name) came out of the ladies room and said, "You won't believe this. There was a bra hanging on the door of my stall." My doctor friend, obviously a veteran of women's rights skirmishes for some time, wryly asked, "Was it burning?"

Dinner was lovely, but I did raise my weak voice again in futile protest of the current raspberry fetish that has gripped the hearts, minds and spatulas of restaurant chefs from sea to shining sea. I haven't eaten out in the last two years without having some raspberry concoction flopped in front of me at the end of the meal. They all seem to delight in splashing some sort of glutinous raspberry sauce over chocolate and Lord knows what else. Failing that, they will lay down a little bed of vanilla pudding and draw EKG trailings in it with lines of raspberry. And, if raspberries are near, I've learned that kiwi fruit can't be far behind. I am urging legislation to limit severely this out-of-control kitchen cliché.

On the way out of the Carter Center, my heart leaped up when I saw in person the long-standing object of my love and lust, political and secular, Geraldine Ferraro. Notwithstanding the fact that we had gotten off to a bad start back in 1984 when I wrote in a column that when I heard her name for the first time I thought someone was referring to Flip Wilson's sports car, I had subsequently corrected my course and publicly avowed my strong feelings for her. She looked absolutely stunning at the Carter Center gathering (picture a scaled-down Babe Zaharias with sex appeal). I have long admitted to an uncontrollable passion for sinewy, dark women in their late forties or early fifties with short, streaked hair, and I would be less than honest if I didn't reveal that when our eyes met I felt that she was sensitive to my deepest feelings in this regard.

Elbowing my way to her side, I waited until our mutual friend, Juanelle Edwards, a progressive Cobb County feminist (that's one who doesn't wear white socks with high heels) could introduce us. Juanelle started off very well saying, "This is Bob Steed, a lawyer and sometime columnist who publicly declared his admiration for you during the 1984 Convention." Just as Geraldine was beginning to warm to my earnest professions of fondness for her, Juanelle popped back in with, "Yes, around here we like to think of Bob as the sex symbol for women who no longer care."

I wish *some* women could be more sensitive.

*February 1988*

# TELL IT ALL, BROTHER!

Like every other reader of suspect moral fiber, I must admit that the recent newspaper accounts on Reverend Jimmy Swaggart's peccadillos struck a prurient chord on my lascivious lyre. I suspect the most fascinating and damaging admission to come out of Reverend Swaggart's confession was the fact that he and the sidewalk stewardess he took to the No-Tell Motel didn't "go all the way" but that he paid her to do some "other things" that were of a pornographic nature.

I think Reverend Swaggart would have been much better advised to confess to a more conventional indiscretion than to leave open to speculation (and the *National Enquirer*) just what in the world those "other things" were. Even the severest of his critics could understand and perhaps forgive a clerical error of the type that so often took place in the Old Testament. I mean those folks in Deuteronomy were always drawing nigh unto one another and begetting to beat the band. But for Swaggart to stop short of coming completely clean was to issue an open invitation to fill in the blank with your darkest fantasy and reminds me of the old story about the country preacher who one Sunday importuned those in his flock to stand up and testify about their sins.

One brother stood up and testified to spending his wages on whiskey rather than tithing, whereupon the preacher shouted, "Tell it all, brother! Tell it all!"

Thus encouraged, the errant parishioner went on to confess that he had been stealing from his employer, and the preacher hooted, "Tell it all, brother! Tell it all!"

Flying to new heights powered by the good that comes to the soul upon confession, the church member then admitted that he had had his way with one of the choir members, and the preacher, in a growing evangelical frenzy, cried, "Tell it all, brother! Tell it *all!*"

Fueled to the ultimate in self-revelatory excess by the preacher's exhortations, the good brother finally blurted out that he had been romantically involved with a goat, to which the preacher exclaimed, "Oh, *brother!* I wouldn't have told *that!*"

In the same connection (perhaps not the right term), I think Rev. Swaggart would have been well advised not to have told that. Having left the door open for all sorts of speculation, there is no telling what folks will come up with as to what was going on during that third-rate romance, low-rent rendezvous.

The mind boggles at all the possibilities, but then my mind boggles so easily. Just a few of the erotic chimeras that flashed upon my x-rated inner eye were as follows:

# THE SASS MENAGERIE

(1)  He paid the young lady to dress in a bikini and violate federal law by tearing tags off the mattresses.

(2)  He paid her to write letters to *Penthouse* magazine over Pat Robertson's name, which he dictated from the Song of Solomon ("While the King was on his couch, my nard gave forth its fragrance. My beloved is to me a bag of myrrh, that lies between my breasts."—Chapter 1, Verses 12 and 13).

(3)  He paid her to join him in watching Ernest Angley on television backwards in the mirror. Or, in the alternative, he tied her up and made her watch Ernest Angley on television. Or (and this is the only way I can watch Ernest Angley) he had her tie him up and made him watch Ernest Angley on television.

(4)  He paid her to put on a wet suit and recreate the Biblical scene where King David watches Bathsheba take a bath while her husband, Uriah, is off doing battle or working down at the Esso Station. (I'm working from memory here.)

(5)  He gets her to use quarters from the church collections to run the Magic Fingers mattress as they listen to his cousin Jerry Lee Lewis's record of "Whole Lotta Shaking Going On."

There's no end to the concupiscent possibilities for someone blessed with a pornographic memory. It's just a matter of, to borrow a stunningly inarticulate modern idiom, whatever turns you on, or, as they used to say in the Song of Solomon days, "Whatever causes your nard to give forth its fragrance."

There may be a lesson here about the consequences of repressive behavior. I can't help but think that none of this would have happened if Reverend Swaggart had been a subscriber to the Playboy Channel. Watching all that stuff gets old in a hurry.

*February 1988*

# HAVE YOU HUGGED YOUR LAWYER TODAY? BUT SERIOUSLY, DOCTOR . . .

I was a bit suspicious when my secretary of twenty years, Yvonne "I didn't go to Marsh Business College for three months to learn how to fetch coffee for you" McMillian, told me that folks from the *Journal of the Medical Association of Georgia* were trying to get in touch with me. Sensing my anxiety, she said soothingly, "Don't worry, they probably just want you to pose for a few photos for an upcoming article on stretch marks."

Notwithstanding her reassuring speculation, it occurred to me that these weren't the best of times for doctors and lawyers in terms of professional relations, and I certainly wasn't eager to put my head in the lion's mouth gratuitously.

When I finally worked up the courage to return the call left by a member of the magazine's publications committee, the distinguished surgeon, J. Rupert "Thumbs" Tillabaugh, I was informed that they wanted a "lighthearted piece that might bring a smile to the lips of readers of the *Journal of the Medical Association of Georgia*." I expressed some reluctance to the good doctor about my ability to lighten or enliven the *Journal*, but he urged me to review a few copies before saying no. After pouring over some scintillating expositions on fascinating subjects ranging from "Symptoms of Irritable Bowel Syndrome" and "The Efficacy of Measuring Bone Mineral Density in Asymptomatic Women: A Preliminary Report" to "Clinical Management of Endocrine Disorders," I decided that perhaps a bit of froth certainly couldn't wreak any permanent havoc and might well punch up the *Journal* for a brief moment.

Filing with Dr. Tillabaugh in advance a caveat that all of my writings were accompanied by some contraindications such as acute fulminations from over-serious readers, oral foaming, involuntary spasms and sputtering on the part of the acutely dignified and sphincter rigidity in those with known sensitivity to feeble attempts at humor, I finally agreed to attempt a piece for the *Journal*.

The thought that doctors (or those who often take themselves more seriously about being doctors than the doctors do themselves, that is, doctors' wives) might take offense at finding an intruder from the legal profession flopping about in the deep and serene waters of the *Journal* gave me some pause, but it was only momentary as I reasoned that I, as a municipal bond attorney, wasn't a real lawyer after all and thus could probably lay claim to more objectivity on the subject of professional relations than someone who actually tried and prosecuted lawsuits. After all, one of my litigator law partners, Byron "Whiplash" Attridge, once described municipal bond attorneys as "people with not enough personality to be tax lawyers but with too much personality to be CPAs."

As someone who has flogged himself around the state addressing bar conventions and medical associations, I have indeed had an opportunity to give thoughtful reflection and temperate expression to the decline in cordiality between the two professions. Frankly, I believe that one of the root causes of this hostile quandary in which we find ourselves locked is a loss of self-esteem among members of both professions. Indeed, who can blame either profession for feeling a slight downward shift in dignity when we find on every cable television channel some huckster lawyer importuning the sick, lame and halt (not to be confused with the small law firm in Marietta by the same name) to drop by for a free consultation on their legal woes or see in every shopping center some Docs-in-a-Box called the "24-Hour EmergiCenter, Ear-Piercing Clinic and Video Rental." Perhaps a return to more dignified times when lawyers wore vests and doctors had unlisted phone numbers would be better for all of us. However, times change, and we must accommodate the change without getting too bitter and resentful about it all.

Of course, I can't speak about the sensitivities of physicians in terms of loss of self-esteem, but in the area of public relations lawyers have long been notorious victims. Throughout history they have been pilloried in song, verse and print by an unforgiving and misunderstanding public. This has, at times, made them jealous and resentful of their brethren in the medical profession.

As a member of that beleaguered brotherhood at the bar, I am always confounded as to why it is that in every public opinion poll ever taken, doctors and specifically surgeons, are always right up there at the top with scientists, astronauts and Mother Teresa, while lawyers find themselves in a knot at the bottom of the pile with used-car salesmen, carnival geeks, chiropractors and Congressmen. After all, the law was a noble

**144**

and enduring profession when medicine involved little more than pulverizing frog eggs, lizard spleens and yak antlers and surgery was still primarily a sideline practiced by barbers.

Some have suggested as a cause for the widespread and notorious unpopularity of lawyers that there are simply too many of us, and, indeed, this is becoming a growing theme for an unrelenting and sensationalist press.

As I have said before in my newspaper column and from the stump, this notion is sheer nonsense. In point of fact, this country at present has only 750,000 lawyers, more or less, with the result that many people don't even have a lawyer of their own but are forced to share one. This is not only inefficient but, depending upon the particular lawyer, often downright unsanitary.

No, even in olden days, when there were far fewer legal practitioners, there was an unreasoning prejudice against lawyers. The drafters of Georgia's original Charter provided that it was to be "a happy, flourishing colony . . . free from [as they diplomatically phrased it] the pest and scourge of mankind known as lawyers." Shakespeare's Dick the Butcher, reacting enthusiastically to Cade's Utopian vision, urged, "The first thing we do, let's kill all the lawyers." Carl Sandburg wrote with malicious and alliterative glee, "Why does the hearse horse snicker when he's hauling a lawyer away?" And even St. Luke, a known physician, took a gratuitous jab in Chapter 11, Verse 46 with "Woe unto ye lawyers also! For you load men with burdens hard to bear, and you yourselves do not touch the burdens with one of your fingers."

Every day seems to bring a new bad joke about lawyers, e.g., "What do you get when you cross a lawyer with a Godfather?" Answer: "Someone who makes you an offer you can't understand."

Some weaker members of the legal profession actually crack under the strain of this bad press. I know a lawyer who drives a bread truck to and from his office in an attempt to

prevent his neighbors from learning the true nature of his day job. Others, when confronted by their sobbing children who have been told by cruel and insensitive playmates that their parent is a lawyer, resort to guile and outright deception, telling their children they are really cocaine traffickers, members of the General Assembly or proctologists.

I have long pointed out to lawyers everywhere that doctors are entirely different in this respect and have a much larger quotient of self-esteem. I tell lawyers that they can learn from practitioners of the healing arts in terms of self-respect. It's simply a matter of self-esteem and pride in their profession. Doctors are *proud* to be doctors. They have little signs on their automobile license plates advertising the fact that they are doctors (this also permits them to park in spaces which would otherwise be reserved for crippled people). At movies, concerts and cocktail parties, doctors happily proclaim their profession by wearing little beepers on their belts like old-time gunslingers. Some of the younger doctors, having noted that typewriter repairmen also wear these beepers, will often go to a public gathering with a stethoscope hanging casually from their pockets just to avoid any confusion. I have seen doctors show up at formal gatherings in black tie, wearing reflectors on their noggins. This does convey a certain panache to an otherwise humdrum outfit.

Moreover, if doctors get into a situation that is so crowded that people are likely to notice neither the electronic beeper nor the dangling stethoscope—a football game, for example—they will simply have themselves paged. I've long advocated having lawyers paged at football games. I think it would help their images tremendously . . . "Lawyer 84, Lawyer 84, please call your office. You missed a mortgage when you checked that last title."

Actually, the doctors are now claiming that there are too many doctors as well. I'd be a little more inclined to accept that claim if all doctors listed their home telephone numbers.

Moreover, you have to make an appointment months in advance to see many specialists, not to mention getting up all the credit references. If an unexpected client happens to wander into a lawyer's office, the lawyer not only sees him right away but generally falls on him like a piranha in a feeding frenzy.

Frankly, my prescription to both lawyers and doctors is nothing more than the wisdom long embodied in Rule 5 of the Kansas General Assembly. This paradigm of good common sense was promulgated by the Kansas General Assembly around the turn of the century and goes simply, "Don't take yourself so damn serious." I am persuaded that if practitioners in both professions would simply take themselves and each other a bit more lightly we would have made a great first stride in getting the proverbial lion and lamb to lie down together. But, in all fairness, I should pass along to the doctors the admonition of that great American philosopher Ralph Waldo Emerson (or maybe it was Shecky Green), who said, "The lion and the lamb may lie down together, but the lamb isn't going to get a hell of a lot of sleep."

*April 1988*

# HE'S BAD

The Democrats have it all wrong. If they want to have any chance at taking back the White House, they need to cut Jesse Jackson loose and start backing Michael Jackson.

This political insight of cosmic consequence came to me at the Omni last Friday evening at the end of Michael Jackson's third Atlanta concert, when, excited, limp and breathless (not to be confused with the sex therapy firm in Marietta by the same name), I turned to my wizened wife, who had dragged me to the event, and said, "That kid is the cat's pajamas."

Walling her eyes and turning to our friends, she said,

"Don't mind him. He still says 'Hubba, hubba' when he sees a pretty girl."

While my words of approbation maybe a trifle dated, my admiration for Michael Jackson is absolutely genuine and up to the minute. I had come to scoff and stayed to praise.

When the three-day concert was announced my entire family—aging rock-'n'-roller wife and three full-time children—began to lobby me to get tickets. Finally, worn down by their shrill importuning, I announced that I would go, but I laid down an ironclad condition that no member of our small party would be permitted to buy one of those cheesy little $2.98 concert T-shirts that unscrupulous promoters palm off on giddy concert goers for seventeen bucks or more. I've found that, if I don't put my foot down from time to time on matters of this nature, chaos reigns.

Michael Jackson, for those gentle readers who may have been locked in a musical coma for the last ten years, is a former black who worked his way up the ladder from cute child group performer to a megastar whose current world tour will net him twenty-nine million U.S. dollars.

My initial reluctance to attend the concert was based on the fact that the offstage Jackson is a little weird for my tastes. First, he is a plastic surgery freak. According to the highly respected *National Enquirer*, he had his nose trimmed so much that there was enough left over to make a new backup singer. He has also had a cleft put in his chin that would make Kirk Douglas twitch in unrestrained envy. Second, he has fits of bizarre behavior offstage, doing things like meditating in an enclosed water tank and trying to buy the remains of the Elephant Man or Harold Stassen's toupee.

However, after sitting through the phantasmagoric, super-surreal show of Jackson's, I was a bona fide fan. With his talent, stage presence and absolutely nuclear energy, I think he would be a superstar even if he had Karl Malden's nose. Incidentally, according to Rona Barrett, Malden is secretly taking moonwalking lessons in a desperate attempt to bolster his sagging career.

The fact that Jackson was not upstaged by all of the high-tech features of his show — laser beams, smoke bombs, thirty-five thousand tons of suspended lights, speakers and other paraphernalia — was in itself a considerable triumph. But rise above the electronic and over-colorful chaos he did. Not only can he sing up a storm, but when it comes to dancing, he looks like Fred Astaire on speed. My operatives tell me that he has installed a practice dance floor in his hotel room. The kid has more moves to his credit that Allied Vans.

Aside from the extraordinary talent, the Star Wars staging and the psychedelic energy, there is an outer-space quality to his concerts that transports the viewers to another dimension.

Around the breakfast table the morning following the concert, musing about the spectacles of the previous evening, my wife, the gnarled neighborhood gnostic, said it all as she sat there over coffee in her cheesy seventeen-dollar Michael Jackson T-shirt. "He is," she observed portentously, "not of this world."

I love it when she talks mystic.

*April 1988*

# CAUSE FOR CONCERN

I found myself wallowing in a slough of despair the other evening (an activity which is not only depressing but, done to excess, can wrinkle the devil out of your suit). When questioned by my querulous spouse as to why I was "moping around," I confided that I was terribly concerned about the lack of new causes these days. I told her that I sensed our country's activists were becoming increasingly jaded with saving the whales, keeping the baby seals from having their ears boxed, fighting Presidential parkways, boycotting lettuce, grapes and the like, and I asked dolefully, "Where are the new areas of cosmic concern coming from?"

"Maybe they should start a campaign to keep people from ending their concerns with prepositions," she sniffed callously, as she dived back into her TV dinner.

By the sheerest of coincidences, the following morning as I sat in my chambers in the grip of a continuing funk, in burst my law partner and friend, Byron "Whiplash" Attridge, waving a sheaf of correspondence that caused my dolorous anxiety to give way to a burst of hope and happiness.

Attridge, while opening his morning mail, had come across a form letter with enclosures that he knew I would find of interest. It was a communiqué from Dr. Merlin D. Tuttle, Founder and Science Director of Bat Conservation International, Inc., thanking Attridge for his "interest in bats" and enclosing valuable information about the threats facing bats here and abroad. Attridge, disclaiming any activist leanings, was puzzled as to how his name got on the mailing list until I reminded him that during his years at Princeton in the 1950s he had led a vigorous protest against the wearing of seersucker suits before Easter and even now was a regular contributor of heated if somewhat incomprehensible letters to the editor deploring the graduated income tax.

Relieved that the nation's best minds were still coming up with fresh causes for our country's ever-eager activists, I plunged happily into Dr. Tuttle's package, and my attention was immediately riveted by a slick brochure featuring a photo of two upside-down bats under Dr. Tuttle's plaintive and rhetorical query, "Why save bats?"

Well, just to ask the question is to answer it. Dr. Tuttle points out that bats are among the most important seed-dispensing animals in the tropical rain forests and have greatly influenced the survival of many fruits, nuts, spices and derivatives from plants such as guavas, carob, peaches and tequila. Frankly, I think some nuts shouldn't survive, or, if they do, they ought to lay off the tequila.

# THE SASS MENAGERIE

Dr. Tuttle, ever the apostle of the obvious, goes on to extol the virtues of bat guano as a major source of fertilizer and then testily debunks a number of common myths about bats by asserting that: (1) they are not rodents; (2) they are not blind and do not "become entangled in people's hair"; and (3) they seldom have rabies. The good doctor carefully avoids mention of some of my primary concerns in the area: (1) that guys with slicked-back hair, capes and black eyeliner often turn themselves into bats and suck the juice out of your neck while you're sleeping; and (2) they are bad to clog up one's belfry.

Lest the unwary should think that bat conservation is only an American dilemma, the BCI letterhead boasts a Scientific Advisory Board with representatives from, among others, Czechoslovakia, India, the UK and, as further evidence of *glasnost*, the redoubtable Dr. Irina K. Rakhmatulina of the USSR. If there is a chapter in Transylvania, no mention is made of it on the letterhead.

Accompanying the letter and brochure is the Bat Conservation International 1987/1988 Catalog featuring an etching of the spotted bat ($50 for non-members; $45 for members), bat jewelry and, of course, bat T-shirts and video cassettes. I kept looking for a catchy bumper sticker saying something like "Lugosi Lives!"

When I excitedly suggested to Attridge that he could leap on the bat bandwagon and, as suggested in the enclosed pledge card, become a supporting member in the thousand-dollar category, he left my office very abruptly. Like, as Dr. Tuttle in his jocular way might say, a bat out of hell.

*June 1988*

155

# RAIL TO
# NO AVAIL

I seem to recall through a glass darkly a statement uttered by Mr. Foster, my Bowdon High School physics teacher in the mid-fifties, to the effect that if a tree fell in the forest and no one was there, it wouldn't make a sound. This utterance so confounded a number of the deep thinkers in our class that Jimmy Ray Ledbetter, who was at the time making one of his infrequent cameo appearances in school, said simply, "That's a damn lie." As Ledbetter outweighed Mr. Foster by some forty pounds and was given to random violence, the critique was allowed to pass unchallenged.

# THE SASS MENAGERIE

The thought came drfiting back to me as I read the swelling list of protesters lining up for the 1988 Democratic Convention. I wondered if there was a protest but no reporters or television cameras were there, would it really be a protest. Such incisive thought is simply part of my nature.

The question, though too metaphysically slithery to grapple with conclusively, is worth some consideration when one ponders the potpourri of protesters now contending for the national spotlight while the convention is in town.

They are a marvelously eclectic lot, and for those gentle readers whose attentions have been distracted by the more mundane and less significant aspects of the convention, i.e., running mates, platforms and the like, I thought it might be useful to have the following summary in one place.

During the convention, the following, among others, are frantically elbowing each other for space on the official protest stomping grounds:

(1) The Don't Shave Anything League — a group of militant feminists who believe that the tradition of shaving any part of the female anatomy is a sexist plot contrived by males to sap the strength of American women. A subcommittee of the group has offered convincing scientific evidence that sustained shaving also causes women to be colder than men, thus causing continuing tension between the sexes over the control of thermostats.

(2) Slave Names Ain't Good (SNAG) — a group of black militants who believe that legislation should be enacted requiring all "slave names" to be abolished and substituting therefor Muslim names such as Mohammed Abdul, Yasir Moussaka, Veal Piccata, Formica Dinette, etc.

(3) The Committee to Bear Arms and Shoot People — a radical spin-off group from the National Rifle Association whose spokesman, "Bubba" Sansaneck, points out, "Hell, what good is it to bear arms if you can't shoot nobody?"

**157**

(4) Jesse Jackson for Vice President Protesters — an unusual mini-rainbow coalition consisting of black activists, street preachers and George Bush supporters.

(5) Presidential Parkway Protesters — a group of anti-Presidential Parkway proponents who claim the proposed parkway to the Carter Library is unnecessary. These folks were going to protest at the Library itself but got lost on the pig trails and side streets that must now be taken to get there.

(6) Gray Gay Panthers — a group of angry old folks who are light in their orthopedic loafers and who are urging their colleagues to come out of nursing home closets across the nation.

(7) The Hiatal Hernia League — a group of militant dyspeptics who believe the government is not putting enough money into hiatal hernia research.

(8) The Save the Newt Alliance — a group of animal conservationists who claim that depletion of the ozone layer presents an increasing threat to the survival of salamanders.

(9) The I-Just-Want-to-Get-on-Television Coalition — a group of generic protesters who have no particular cause and whose primary goal is to hoot and holler in front of television cameras for no apparent reason. They plan to offer Rev. Hosea Williams as a third-party Presidential candidate if they can get collision insurance for the campaign bus.

(10) Freedom Over Our Bodies Sisterhood — a group of pro-choice advocates who believe that abortion rights should be extended so as to permit women to have an abortion any time prior to the time the child leaves for college. Some hard-liners within the group believe that the right to abortion should continue during college if the child fails to maintain a *C* average or better.

## THE SASS MENAGERIE

There are a number of other splinter groups contending for space in the spotlight as well, but as their causes are, in my judgment, somewhat frivolous, I am making no mention of them in this dispatch.

All of this might cause one to wonder if Shakespeare (I think it was Shakespeare; it could have been Judge Wapner) was right when he said, "Methinks they doth protest too much."

*July, 1988*

# I'LL GET BY AS LONG AS I HAVE YOU

August 23, 1988, marks the thirtieth year since my sinewy spouse and I jumped the broomstick on a hot and hazy day in a tasteful double-ring ceremony in Bowdon, Georgia. The better element in Bowdon still recalls in admiring tones the lavish reception staged by the proud parents of the bride at the Greyhound Bus Station in Carrollton, where friends and relatives gorged themselves on cheese straws and Spam canapeś surrounding an imitation cut-glass punch bowl in which a large block of lime sherbert floated sluggishly in a sea of ginger ale. The father of the bride was heard to say, "Damn the expense; these are my friends."

Notwithstanding the fact that this union, widely acknowledged to be a mismatch across social and class lines, has endured for three decades, there still are those who enthusiastically accuse me of saying and writing "rude and insensitive things" about my wiry wife. Most often, my accusers are militant feminists who some years back took umbrage at my pronouncement that the term "militant feminists" was, itself, a redundancy. (For those gentle readers who have never actually seen a militant feminist taking umbrage, I would point out that it is not a pretty sight.)

I, of course, vigorously and vehemently deny these allegations, pointing out that I would never say anything rude or insensitive about my bride for a number of reasons. First, she's mean as a snake, vicious, cunning and cruel, and, second, as any husband with a grain of sense knows, there comes a time in every twenty-four-hour day when the husband is in bed asleep while the wife is still up stalking about. If the husband has truly gotten crossways in the stream with the wife, she can seize upon that unhappy moment to take up some blunt or, worse yet, sharp instrument and do him some grievous bodily harm.

There is a story, perhaps apocryphal, illustrating this unhappy possibility. It is said that Willie Nelson, in another life with an earlier wife, came home in a state so besotted that he appeared to be walking on a trampoline and made some rude and insensitive remarks to his then-wife. The good lady kept her peace until Willie went to bed, whereupon she took a needle and thread and sewed him up in the bottom sheet and then gave him a wake-up call with a pick handle. A chastened Nelson later described the episode saying, "Imagine waking up in a sea of white and a world of pain. It looked like heaven but felt like hell."

There are ample reasons beyond the fear of marital mayhem that keep me from uttering rude and insensitive things about my wife. On the contrary, she has many admirable qualities which, looking back from the perspective of thirty years together, I recognize, admire and esteem.

To list just a few by way of public tribute (and with the hope that this written offering will suffice as an anniversary present), I offer the following:

(1) She can still wear the wedding dress she crafted with her own hands in 1958 while I would not be able to get into my dark blue wash-and-wear suit by Haspel with a large shoehorn and a can of Crisco.

(2) She still looks good in a bikini while I was recently asked by a lifeguard to either get a top to my bathing suit or leave the beach.

(3) She is one of the most energetic housekeepers ever to polish a plant leaf. Many is the time when I have gotten up in the middle of the evening to go to the bathroom and returned to find my side of the bed made up. Moreover, she has a deep-seated urge to Windex things that borders on compulsion. She is forever on the prowl with a spray bottle of the stuff, squirting it on counter surfaces, stoves, shelves, refrigerators and all manner of appliances and once Windexed a torpid houseguest who made the mistake of staying in one spot too long. He recommended we put her on the waiting list at the Betty Ford Center for Ammonia Abuse.

(4) She is possessed of physical courage rare in one so slight and old. The woman is absolutely fearless. She will fly parachutes at the beach, ride hot-air balloons in foreign countries, has gone to Egypt and Africa without me and once voluntarily witnessed an autopsy. I, on the other hand, send her downstairs to investigate things that go bump in the night

and was almost eighteen before I would ride anything on the merry-go-round other than the bench.

(5) She is a wonderful winner in gin games, and on the infrequent occasions when she bests me in a hand, she will show her teeth in a superior way and snort and chortle relentlessly.

(6) She has a persistence and single-mindedness that I particularly admire. For example, she has been reading the same novel since high school. Every evening she will work elaborately on making a little reading nest on her side of the bed with pillow plumping and arranging and positioning of the lamp, finally settling in for some sustained reading. Two minutes later almost to the second, I hear labored breathing and look over to see her in what appears to be a serious coma, having knocked off another page and a half of *Forever Amber*.

(7) She is the most energetic and resourceful provider of malapropisms I have ever encountered. Just the other evening when describing a friend, she said the woman could "talk the hounds off a billy goat." More recent than that, while discussing a portrait she was painting, she was a party to the following exchange:

**She:** I'm going to put a flag in that painting, but it's got to be "obsteturous."
**Me:** What do you mean by "obsteturous"?
**She:** Well, obsteturous means "in the way," so I guess I should have said "unobsteturous."

The conversation continued, but by that time I was so dizzy and my head hurt so that I am unable to recall the balance of the colloquy.

I could go on, but the point is that I believe that every truly sensitive husband, like myself, should occasionally (at least every thirty years) count and catalog his marital blessings and, beyond that, should publicly acknowledge them. This would go a long way toward holding down the rampant divorce rate now galloping through our connubial ranks.

When asked by others about the longevity of our imperfect union, I often quote Paul Newman, another lifer in the marriage game, who, answering the same query, said, "Think of murder but never divorce."

I think of murder every time she snorts and chortles over a winning gin hand, but, with luck, I hope to hang in there for at least another thirty, and, in the meantime, borrowing the words of a Dick Haymes song popular in the 1940s, I publicly proclaim to the one whose heavy-lidded gaze still causes heavy breathing on my part, "I'll Get By as Long as I Have You."

*August 1988*

# About the Author

Robert L. Steed is an Atlanta attorney and a dilettante columnist for the *Atlanta Constitution*. A native of Bowdon, Georgia, he is married to the former Linda Ruth McElroy, a painter whom he describes as "101 pounds of grit, gristle and ingratitude." They are the parents of three children — Joshua, Georgia and Nona Begonia. Steed is the author of three previous books: *Willard Lives!*, *Lucid Intervals* and *Money, Power and Sex (A Self-Help Guide for All Ages)*. Former U.S. Attorney General Griffin Bell says of Steed, "His ego is such that he has group photos taken of himself." Pat Conroy calls him "the funniest legal mind since Richard Nixon." He is generally acknowledged to be the funniest lawyer not presently serving time.

# About the Illustrator

Jack Davis grew up in Atlanta with a notorious group — later characterized as the "Buckhead Boys"—that included William Emerson and James Dickey. He attended the University of Georgia and the Art Students League of New York. During his career as an illustrator and cartoonist, he has spanned the world for *Mad Magazine* and continues as one of *Mad*'s regular and most popular contributors.

His illustrations have graced ads of all descriptions, movie posters, record covers, Topps baseball cards, books, magazines and magazine covers, including *TV Guide* and, at last count, thirty-six covers of *Time*. He also illustrated Steed's previous books, *Lucid Intervals* and *Money, Power and Sex (A Self-Help Guide for All Ages)*.

An avid University of Georgia football fan, Davis is the creator of the belligerent and zany-looking bulldog on billboards, athletic programs and other UGA paraphernalia.

He and his wife, Dena, live in Hartsdale, New York, but will soon return to Georgia, where they are building a home on St. Simons Island.